America's Neighborhood Bats

*Understanding and Learning to Live
in Harmony with Them*

MERLIN D. TUTTLE

AMERICA'S
NEIGHBORHOOD
BATS

 UNIVERSITY OF TEXAS PRESS, AUSTIN

Unless otherwise noted, photographs are by Merlin D. Tuttle.

Frontispiece: a Sanborn's long-nosed bat (Leptonycteris sanborni) about to pollinate a saguaro cactus flower. Its face is already covered with pollen from a visit to another flower and will soon disappear into this one, transferring pollen from one flower to another. Saguaro flowers open at night, produce special odors, and are perfectly shaped to fit a bat's head. This and other giant cacti of the Southwest rely heavily on these bats for pollination, but the bats are now endangered. Their loss threatens the survival of giant cacti which, in turn, threatens the future of entire southwestern desert ecosystems. This situation is echoed throughout the world in many other environments.

Copyright © 1988
by the University of Texas Press

All rights reserved

Printed in Japan

Second Printing, 1989

Requests for permission to reproduce material from this work should be sent to: Permissions, University of Texas Press, Box 7819, Austin, Texas 78713-7819.

Library of Congress Cataloging-in-Publication Data

Tuttle, Merlin D.
  America's neighborhood bats.
  Bibliography: p.
  Includes index.
  1. Bats — United States.   2. Bats — Social aspects — United States.   3. Mammals — United States.   4. Mammals — Social aspects — United States.   I. Title.
QL737.C5T88   1988   599.4'0973   88-10696
ISBN 0-292-70403-8
ISBN 0-292-70406-2 (pbk.)

CONTENTS

*To Bill Walker, president and chief executive officer,
Bacardi Imports, Inc., in recognition of his exemplary
efforts on behalf of bat conservation*

ACKNOWLEDGMENTS

Indian flying fox (Pteropus *giganteus*), *perched.*

I thank Bacardi Imports, Inc., Miami, Florida, for its generous grant in support of this book as well as for decades of efforts to educate the public about bats and their value. I also deeply appreciate the many members of Bat Conservation International, whose financial support of my research and conservation efforts helped make this book possible. Of these, I am especially indebted to John and Anne Earhart, Bill Haber, John Mitchell, Verne and Marion Read, Sally Smyth, and Christine Stevens. The Chapman Foundation and the Richmond Area Speleological Society also played a key role in making this work possible, and I thank Bat Conservation International trustees Arthur Brown, Donald Grantges, Ellen King, John Mitchell, George Perry, Peggy Phillips, Verne Read, D. J. Sibley, Jr., Gordon Sears, and Bill Walker for their constant encouragement.

I am grateful to Bat Conservation International staff members Mari Murphy and Dr. Paul Robertson for their substantial editorial assistance and to Cindy Lind for secretarial help. I also am indebted to the following colleagues for their invaluable reviews and extensive suggestions: Dr. Denny Constantine, public health veterinarian, California Department of Health Services; Dr. Stephen Frantz, rodent and bat specialist, Wadsworth Center for Laboratories and Research, State of New York Department of Health; Dr. Thomas Kunz, chairman, Department of Biology, Boston University; Dr. Charles Rupprecht, assistant professor, Rabies Research Unit, Wistar Institute.

Earl Johnson, area manager, Minnesota Department of Natural Resources, Detroit Lakes, provided a photograph and information about bat house success in Minnesota. Text drawings are by Charles Shaw, key drawings by Priscilla Vogt, and range maps by Josie Cox.

For Additional Information

Educational publications and programs, books
about bats, bat houses, and other items are available
from Bat Conservation International, a nonprofit
membership organization. Members receive the
quarterly publication, *Bats,* authored by leading experts who write at the layman's level. The organization's purpose is to document and publicize the
value and conservation needs of bats, to promote
conservation and research projects, and to assist
with management initiatives worldwide. For a
catalog and membership information, write:

Bat Conservation International
P.O. Box 162603
Austin, TX 78716

Introduction

This book has been slowly taking shape in my mind for some 20 years, stimulated by countless phone calls from needlessly frightened, often panicked people who had just discovered one or more bats in their home or yard. My purpose is to introduce these frequently misunderstood animals to the layman, to provide solutions to problems, to dispel unnecessary fears, and to encourage an appreciation of bats and their conservation needs.

Fear of things we understand the least is a well-documented aspect of human behavior, and that is precisely the problem faced by bats. Numerous myths and superstitions have persisted because the real lives of bats are so poorly known. Health concerns that we should have and cautions that we should observe for bats are the same as those we should apply to most wild animals. It is my hope that this book will help to resolve some of the striking conflicts between the myth and reality of bats.

Some of the most commonly asked questions are: "Is it rabid?" "Will it attack or hurt me?" "What should I do?" My usual response is to ask the person to describe the problem. This is often puzzling to callers, because they think that I, of all people, should know that the mere presence of a bat constitutes a serious problem! I sympathize with people who suffer as a result of needless fear, but I must admit that I find many of their stories quite comical.

One morning, as I was walking down the hall toward my office, I heard the phone ringing incessantly. When I answered, a woman, so frightened that she could barely speak, told me that she and her husband were barricaded in their home and insisted that they were surrounded by attacking bats that had "nearly gotten them" when they had returned home the previous evening. They had spent most of the night trying to plug every possible entry and didn't dare leave the house. A few quick questions revealed that the culprits were actually migrating monarch butterflies that had spent the night resting in their yard. The mere possibility of bats had caused the most terrifying night of their lives.

In a similar case of misidentification, a county park superintendent demanded that I tell him immediately how to find bat "nests" so he could eradicate all bats living in or near his park. He claimed that four people had been attacked by rabid bats in a single week and that the county was about to be sued for failure to protect its citizens. The people in question were already taking the then painful rabies inoculations. My investigation revealed that the culprit was a screech owl guarding her nest. She was striking people on the head as they walked beneath her tree at dusk. By the time the startled victims looked around, all they could see were the silhouettes of flying bats while the owl sat hidden in the tree. Even though all of these incidents had occurred under the same tree, and despite our demonstration that there was a protective mother screech owl in the tree, one of the victims insisted on continuing the shots because he said he grew up on a farm and knew a bat when he saw one!

Once I was even asked to investigate a bat "mauling." A workman in a Tennessee Valley Authority dam claimed that he had been attacked by bats and that they had seriously lacerated his arm when he reached into a locker where they were roosting. He was rushed to a doctor, who believed his story, and immediately began rabies inoculations. When I arrived,

Dr. Merlin Tuttle and a friend from Australia. Susie is an orphaned Greyheaded flying fox.

frightened workmen were refusing to reenter the dam until they could be certain that all bats had been evicted. I met the injured man, who assured me that he had been attacked, but I knew at a glance that bats could not have inflicted such serious damage. My investigation was complicated by the man's anger, from my doubting his account, and by the fearful reluctance of his coworkers to guide me to the scene of the alleged attack. Eventually, I was able to catch one of the bats and demonstrate to the man's satisfaction that the species involved was literally incapable of breaking human skin with its tiny teeth. We then visited the locker, where I showed that a piece of unfinished metal on the inside of the locker had scratched his arm when he yanked it out in a panic. By the time I left, he was furious at the doctor for believing his story and giving him the shots!

In another instance, a family that had neglected to close windows at their summer cottage called from a motel one morning after they were panicked by a small colony of little brown bats that had taken advantage of their absence. On the previous night, after the bats had left to feed, the family had returned to the cottage and gone to bed. At 2 A.M. they awakened to find several dozen bats flying around their bedrooms. They fled in their pajamas, hiking several miles to the nearest farmhouse, where they were told that once bats had established their odor, the only remedy for getting rid of them was to burn the house down. They were extremely relieved to learn that they had been misinformed.

Unbridled fear of bats can be far more dangerous than bats themselves. For example, people have broken legs in frantic "escapes," nearly drowned when they fell off boat docks in reaction to bats in hot pursuit of mosquitoes, and I know of one instance in which an entire home was demolished when a gas fumigant exploded while being used to exterminate bats. Suffice it to say, people need answers to their questions about neighborhood bats.

The World of Bats

Bat fossils have been found that date back approximately 50 million years, but, surprisingly, the bats of that ancient period very closely resembled those we know today. Thus, bats have been around for a very long time. Before humans began to affect their numbers, bats were extremely abundant. In some places they probably dominated the night skies just as passenger pigeons filled the daytime skies of the eastern United States prior to the nineteenth century. In the evolution of nature's system of checks and balances, bats long have played an essential role; their loss today could compromise the health and stability of our environment.

Bats are mammals, but such unique ones that scientists have placed them in a group of their own, the Chiroptera, which means hand-wing. All living bat species fit into one of two major groups, the Microchiroptera or the Megachiroptera. Members of the latter group are commonly referred to as flying foxes because of their foxlike faces. They are found only in the Old World tropics, while the Microchiroptera, which are highly varied in appearance, occur worldwide.

Like humans, bats give birth to poorly developed young and nurse them from a pair of pectoral breasts. In fact, Linnaeus, the father of modern taxonomy, was so impressed by the similarities between bats and primates (lemurs, monkeys, apes, and humans) that he originally put them into the same taxonomic group. Today's scientists generally agree that primates and bats share a common shrewlike ancestor, but belong to separate groups.

A heated debate was recently triggered by the discovery that flying foxes, primates, and flying lemurs share a unique brain organiza-

Nearly a thousand species of bats come in an amazing variety of appearances, some being as distantly related as a grizzly bear is to a sea otter. From left to right, top to bottom: Straw-colored flying fox (Eidolon helvum), *equatorial Africa;* Sanborn's long-nosed bat (Leptonycteris sanborni), *Central America to southwestern United States;* Townsend's big-eared bat (Plecotus townsendii), *mostly western North America;* southern yellow bat (Lasiurus ega), *southwestern United States to South America;* hoary bat (Lasiurus cinereus), *North and South America;* Franquet's flying fox (Epomops franqueti), *equatorial Africa;* tent-making bat (Uroderma bilobatum), *southern Mexico to South America;* Peter's ghost-faced bat (Mormoops megalophylla), *southwestern United States to Central America;* evening bat (Nycticeius humeralis), *central and eastern United States to Mexico;* spotted bat (Euderma maculatum), *western North America.*

tion. (Flying lemurs, apparently close relatives of the true lemurs of Madagascar, are a poorly known group of cat-size gliding mammals that live in the Indonesian region and, like bats, are in a separate group of their own, the Dermoptera.) Did both the Micro- and Megachiroptera come from a single, shrewlike, gliding ancestor, or did the flying foxes evolve separately from primates? If the latter notion is correct, are their unique brain characteristics sufficient reason for reclassifying flying lemurs and flying foxes as primates? The issue remains unresolved, but most scientists agree that bats are far more closely related to primates than to the rodents with which they often are linked in the public mind.

DIVERSITY AND DISTRIBUTION
The nearly one thousand kinds of bats amount to approximately a quarter of all mammal species, and they are found everywhere except in the most extreme desert and polar regions. Some forty species live in the United States and Canada, but the majority inhabit tropical forests where, in total number of species, they sometimes outnumber all other mammals combined.

Bats come in an amazing variety of sizes and appearances. The world's smallest mammal, the bumblebee bat of Thailand, weighs less than a penny, but some flying foxes of the Old World tropics have wingspans of up to 6 feet. The big-eyed, winsome expressions of flying foxes often surprise people who would never have thought that a bat could be attractive. Some bats have long angoralike fur, ranging in color from bright red or yellow to jet black or white. One species is furless, and another even has pink wings and ears. A few are so brightly patterned that they are known as butterfly bats.

Agave plants, from which tequila is produced, are so dependent on bats for pollination that without them, the probability of successful seed production drops to one three-thousandth of normal.

Others have enormous ears, nose leaves, and intricate facial features that may seem bizarre at first, but become more fascinating than strange when their sophisticated role in navigation is explained.

NAVIGATION AND MIGRATION

Like dolphins, most bats communicate and navigate with high-frequency sounds. Using sound alone, these bats can "see" everything but color, and in total darkness they can detect obstacles as fine as a human hair. The sophistication of their unique echolocation systems surpasses current scientific understanding and on a watt-per-watt, ounce-per-ounce basis has been estimated to be literally billions of times more efficient than any similar system developed by humans. In addition, bats are not blind and many have excellent vision.

In temperate regions, cold winters force bats to migrate or hibernate. Most travel less than 300 miles to find a suitable cave or abandoned mine, where they remain for up to six months or more, surviving solely on stored fat reserves. However, several species are long-distance migrators, traveling from as far north as Canada to the Gulf states or Mexico for the winter. A few species can survive short-term exposure to subfreezing temperatures, enabling them to overwinter in cliff faces or in the outer walls of buildings.

Typically, bats are very loyal to their birthplaces and hibernating sites, but how they find their way over the long distances that often exist between their hibernating and feeding areas remains largely a mystery. It appears that some orient visually, using mountain ranges and other landmarks to guide them, but a few are known to have found their way even when

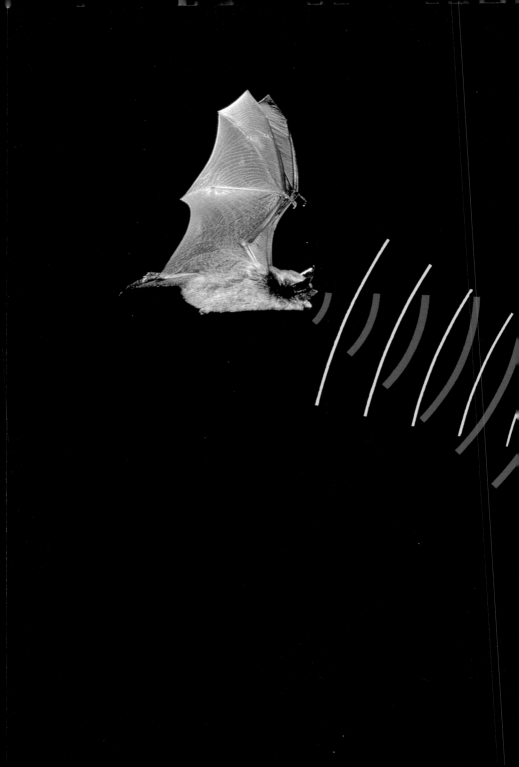

Hunting bats detect prey by echolocation. A bat emits high-frequency sounds that bounce back to its ears, enabling it to detect objects as fine as a human hair in total darkness.

blinded. Information about how to find obscure sites, such as small cave entrances, apparently is passed on from generation to generation.

COURTSHIP, REPRODUCTION, AND LONGEVITY
Most bats that live in temperate regions, such as the United States and Canada, mate in the fall just before entering hibernation. As far as we know, there is very little courting, and males are generally promiscuous, mating with as many females as possible. Ovulation and fertilization (through sperm that have been dormant in the female reproductive tract since the previous fall) occur in the spring as females emerge from hibernation. Pregnant females then move from hibernating sites (hibernacula) to warmer roosts, where they form nursery colonies. Birth occurs approximately a month and a half to two months later. The young grow rapidly, often learning to fly within three weeks. While they are being reared, males and nonreproductive females often segregate into separate groups called bachelor colonies.

Some tropical bats engage in elaborate courtship displays. For example, male epauleted bats sing and flash large fluffs of white shoulder fur to attract mates, while male crested bats perform a spectacular display by expanding long hairs on top of the head, similar to a peacock spreading its tail. At least a few tropical species are monogamous, sharing hunting and family duties. Vampire bats even adopt orphans, unusual for any wild animal.

Bats are, for their size, the slowest reproducing mammals on earth. On average, mother bats rear only one young per year, and some do not give birth until they are two or more years old. Exceptionally long-lived, a few may survive for more than 30 years.

FEEDING AND ROOSTING BEHAVIOR

Although 70 percent of bats eat insects, many tropical species feed exclusively on fruit or nectar. A few are carnivorous, hunting small vertebrates, such as fish, frogs, mice, and birds. Despite their notoriety, vampire bats make up only a small portion of all bats (there are only three species), and they live only in Latin America. With the exception of three species of nectar-feeding bats that live along the Mexican border of Arizona and Texas, all bats in the United States and Canada are insectivorous.

Bats can be found living in almost any conceivable shelter, though they are best known for living in caves. Many species that now live mostly in buildings do so, at least in part, because they have few alternatives. Tropical species occupy a wider range of roost sites than temperate species. For example, some make tentlike roosts by biting through the midribs of large leaves, and several species have suction discs on their wings and feet that enable them to live in the slick-walled cavities formed by unfurling leaves, such as those of the banana plant. Others live in animal burrows, flowers, termite nests, and even in large tropical spider webs. Despite the wide variety of roosts used by bats, many species have adapted to living in roosts of only one or a few types and cannot survive anywhere else.

ECOLOGICAL AND ECONOMIC VALUE

Worldwide, bats are the major predators of night-flying insects, a category that includes mosquitoes and numerous crop pests. Individual mouse-eared bats, the most widely distributed of North American bat species, can catch up to 600 mosquitoes in an hour, and large colonies of bats consume countless bil-

lions of insects each season. The 20 million free-tailed bats from Bracken Cave in Central Texas, eat a quarter of a million pounds or more of insects in a single night!

Throughout the tropics the seed dispersal and pollination activities of fruit- and nectar-eating bats are vital to the survival of rain forests, with some bats acting as "keystone" species in the lives of plants crucial to entire ecosystems. Many plants bloom at night, using unique odors and special flower shapes to attract bats. The famous baobab tree of the eastern African savannas is a good example. Only bats approach from below in a manner likely to contact the flower's reproductive organs and achieve pollination. Of course they do so because the plant rewards them handsomely with nectar. This tree is so important to the survival of other kinds of wildlife that it is often referred to as the "Tree of Life."

Pictured at right is a Jamaican fruit-eating bat (**Artibeus jamaicensis**). *Seeds dispersed by bats are vital to reforestation of tropical rain forests. Bats may drop up to 95 percent of the seeds that produce the first "pioneer" plants in a clearing. These plants then shelter less hardy species that later attract birds and larger mammals, who in turn aid in developing the incredible plant diversity for which rain forests are famous.*

A pallid bat (Antrozous pallidus) *carries a katydid back to its night roost before feeding. These bats are important predators of grasshoppers, katydids, crickets and centipedes.*

Wild varieties of many of the world's most economically valuable crop plants also rely on bats for survival. Some of the better known commercial products are fruits such as bananas, breadfruit, avocados, dates, figs, peaches, and mangoes. Others include cloves, cashews, carob, balsa wood, kapok (filler for life preservers), and even tequila. Most of the plants from which these products come are now commercially cultivated, but the maintenance of wild ancestral stocks is critically important. They are the only source of genetic material for developing disease-resistant strains, rejuvenating commercial varieties, and for producing new, more productive plants in the future.

We already know that more than 300 plant species in the Old World tropics alone rely on the pollinating and seed dispersal services of bats, and additional bat-plant relationships are constantly being discovered. These plants provide more than 450 economically important products, valued in the hundreds of millions of dollars annually. Just one, the durian fruit of Southeast Asia, sells for $120 million each year and relies almost exclusively on flying foxes for pollination. Other products from these 300-plus plants include 110 for food and drinks, 72 for medicines, 66 for timber and wood derivatives, 34 for ornamentals, 29 for fiber and cordage, 25 for dyes, 19 for tannins, 11 for animal fodder, and 8 for fuel. Numerous additional bat-dependent plants of the New World tropics are of similarly great importance.

The value of tropical bats in reforestation alone is enormous. Seeds dropped by bats can account for up to 95 percent of forest regrowth on cleared land. Performing this essential role puts these bats among the most important seed-dispersing animals of both the Old and New World tropics.

Studies of bats have contributed to the development of navigational aids for the blind, birth control and artificial insemination techniques, vaccine production, and drug testing, as well as to a better understanding of low-temperature surgical procedures. Unfortunately, however, careless exploitation of bats has sometimes decimated local populations, and careful management planning is required.

Resolving Misconceptions

UNDERSTANDING OUR FEARS

Bats are feared only to the extent that they are misunderstood. In Asia and the Pacific Islands, where flying foxes have wingspans of 3 to 6 feet and live conspicuously in the treetops like birds, no one fears them. They are actually depicted as heroes in some Pacific Island legends, and in China they are held in high esteem as omens of good luck and happiness. In contrast, in America and Europe, where all bats are small and difficult to observe, they are often intensely feared and persecuted. Our ignorance is frequently embellished with a great deal of myth and superstition. For example, people believe bats are blind and that they become entangled in people's hair. Neither is true. Although diseases have been better studied in bats than in most other animals, only two, rabies and histoplasmosis, are known to have been transmitted by them to humans, and our fears of acquiring even these from bats are often grossly exaggerated.

FACTS ABOUT RABIES

Like most mammals, bats can contract rabies; however, it is a common misconception that most bats are rabid. This impression stems from early studies that seemed to show that, unlike other animals, bats could survive rabies infection and transmit the disease over long periods of time without showing any signs of sickness themselves. This belief gave rise to the suspicion that large numbers of bats were acting as asymptomatic carriers, serving as disease reservoirs for other animals. The presumption that they were asymptomatic carriers of rabies received worldwide publicity and quickly became entrenched in nearly everyone's mind as fact.

However, more than 20 years of subsequent research tells a very different story.

Less than a half of 1 percent of bats contract rabies, a frequency no higher than that seen in many other animals. Like others, they die quickly, but unlike even dogs and cats, rabid bats seldom become aggressive. Rabies experts now believe that many of the bats believed rabid in early studies were actually infected with another agent, such as Rio Bravo virus, that is harmless to bats and people but fatal to mice. When tissue isolates from rabies-free but Rio Bravo–infected bats were inoculated into mice, the mice died of rabieslike signs, leading to the erroneous conclusion that the bats were asymptomatic rabies carriers.

Subsequent studies, covering wide geographic areas and comparing the frequency of rabies in other wildlife with the abundance of bats, have consistently shown just the opposite of what would be expected if bats were important reservoirs for rabies outbreaks (i.e., there were fewer, not more, cases of rabies in other wildlife where bats were most abundant). In fact, even when rabid bats were forced to bite a wide variety of laboratory animals — dogs, cats, skunks, raccoons, and foxes — the subjects rarely contracted the disease. Recent studies involving wildlife rabies virus strain comparisons permit identification of the potential animal source from which the disease originated, confirming the belief that rabid bats seldom transmit rabies to any animals except other bats. In the few instances in which rabies has been transmitted from a bat to a cat or fox, the infected individual apparently died without causing an outbreak.

Dr. Denny Constantine, a public health veterinarian for the state of California, is one of the world's leading authorities on the public health implications of rabies in bats. He has inspected more sick bats than anyone else in North America. Writing in response to an inquiry regarding bats and public health, he placed the danger in perspective as follows:

The public health problems posed by bats are relatively insignificant compared to the public health problems usually initiated by those who publicize bats as problematic, typically resulting in an exaggerated, inappropriate public response, damaging to the public health.

My recent survey work in California indicates that only about one in a thousand bats may be incubating rabies; the infected animal will soon become paralyzed and die. Rabies-infected house bats and most other bats in the United States do not experience outbreaks of rabies; instead, only an occasional animal becomes infected. The lack of savage attacks and lack of outbreaks contrasts with the rabies problem in skunks and foxes, for example. Thus, bat rabies is far less hazardous than anyone would ordinarily expect it to be. . . .

Information concerning bats is usually misinterpreted through stimulation of one's imagination, influenced by folklorish misconceptions that transform reality into an exciting tale everyone will listen to. For example, bats that dart by persons to eat mosquitoes are often accused of trying to attack the people instead. Even public health workers often unhesitatingly accept such misinterpretations. Given this predisposition, the public generally will accept, if not embellish, any story or half-truth concerning bats that is suggested.

According to Dr. Constantine, reports of high rates of rabies in bats usually occur because of sampling biases. For example, most labs test only bats that are submitted because they are rabies-suspect. Results are often reported in the media in a manner that implies that these bats are representative of bats in general. An ex-

treme case involved a claim that 50% of a state's bats were rabid because one of only two bats examined tested positive.

RABIES PREVENTION

Vaccination of dogs and cats is the most important action that can be taken to protect the public from exposure to rabies. Even in urban settings pets come into contact with wild and feral animals that can be infected. Also, it is essential that people, especially children, be cautioned about the potential dangers of contact with unfamiliar animals. They should be warned that any bat that can be caught is more likely than others to be sick and that it should not be handled. The same caution applies to all wild mammals. Even among sick bats, the vast majority is not rabid, but one should not take unnecessary chances with a fatal disease. In the event of any animal bite medical advice should be sought immediately. Strictly following these precautions will make the danger of contracting rabies incalculably small.

Aerosol (through the air) transmission of rabies is rare. It has been reported only under unusual circumstances in rabies research laboratories and in two caves where air in very humid environments was saturated with vapors created by tens of millions of bats — a unique situation to say the least. Only two humans are believed to have contracted rabies through such aerosol transmission, but caution in poorly ventilated caves occupied by millions of bats is advisable. Thousands of people explore other less densely populated bat caves each year, and none has contracted rabies as a result. There is no evidence to suggest such danger in buildings.

Bats that can be caught, especially those found on the ground or in unusual places, are far more likely than others to be sick. For this reason, they should not be handled without leather work gloves, and children, in particular, should be warned never *to pick up bats.*

Casual contact, such as merely touching a rabid animal, does not constitute exposure unless scratches, abrasions, open wounds, or mucous membranes contact potentially infectious material, such as the animal's saliva or nervous tissue. This includes touching one's mouth, nose, or eyes after handling infected material. There is no evidence that bat rabies can be transmitted to humans through contact with urine or feces, and anyone bitten is usually aware of the fact at the time.

If one is exposed, the site should be immediately washed with soap and water, and medical advice sought. It is comforting to know that the old series of injections in the stomach is no longer necessary. The modern rabies vaccine is relatively painless, very effective, and one of the safest inoculations available. Treatment requires just six shots, one of human rabies immune globulin and five doses of vaccine in the arm. Preexposure immunity can be obtained with only three injections and is recommended for anyone who is regularly in contact with potentially infected wildlife.

HISTOPLASMOSIS

Histoplasmosis is a disease caused by a fungus, *Histoplasma capsulatum,* that prefers soils enriched by bird or bat droppings. Human infection occurs through breathing dust that contains contaminated spores. Symptoms normally include a cough and are flulike. Throughout wide areas of the Americas, Europe, Africa, and the Far East, up to 80 percent of the human population has been exposed. Bird droppings, frequently those of poultry or pigeons, are the primary source of infection for people. The fungus is occasionally present, but uncommon, in droppings found in hot, dry attics where bats roost. Ninety percent of cases in the United States are reported from the Ohio and Mississippi river drainages and east into Virginia and Maryland. It is rare in the northern states and Canada. Aside from a few virulent forms from caves, especially in Latin America and Africa, infections are usually asymptomatic. Serious illness seldom results.

The severity of histoplasmosis infection normally is directly proportional to the amount of dust-laden spores inhaled. To avoid problems, do not stir up and breathe dust in areas where bird or bat droppings have accumulated. If removal of droppings is necessary, use of a properly fitted respirator, capable of filtering particles as small as two microns in diameter, will greatly reduce the probability of exposure.

PARASITES

Like all mammals, bats may harbor fleas, mites, or ticks. Fortunately, bat parasites are highly host specific, which means that they rarely bite people or pets. Despite intensive research, no bat parasite has been shown to transmit any disease to humans. Dr. Constantine has written, "I have been working in bat roosts in buildings for some 45 years, and I've never been aware of a bite from a bug or anything else." He notes that although isolated reports exist, he "would expect such bites to be exceedingly rare." Most parasites that remain after their hosts depart soon die.

PUTTING DANGERS IN PERSPECTIVE

I have personally studied bats worldwide for 25 years, including hundreds of species and tens of thousands of individuals, spending weeks at a time photographing colonies numbering as many as 20 million. I have never seen an aggressive bat, nor have I contracted a disease from a bat. Since the recent development of an effective rabies vaccine, I have availed myself of this protection, as anyone who regularly handles wildlife should.

In more than four decades, public health records indicate that only 16 people in the United States and Canada have died of bat-borne diseases, 15 from rabies and 1 from histoplasmosis. Placed in perspective, this means that the odds of anyone dying of a disease from a bat are much less than one in a million. In contrast, in the United States alone more than 10 people die *annually* from dog attacks, not to mention dog- and cat-transmitted diseases, honey bee stings, or food poisoning contracted at picnics. For people who simply do not handle bats, there is little cause for worry.

MISINFORMATION AND ITS CONSEQUENCES

Dr. Constantine and other authorities repeatedly have warned that the worst public health hazards associated with bats are those created when needlessly panicked people are exploited by an unscrupulous pest control company in the guise of saving them from bats. Writing in an effort to curb such misinformation, he has pointed out that such companies contribute news items and general information to the media and "that misconceptions concerning bat rabies have been disseminated in this manner, creating a self-perpetuating cycle of hysteria."

A second problem occasionally involves public health officials themselves. Most are aware of the hazards created by panic and now provide sound advice. Unfortunately, a vocal few continue to make exaggerated claims that the news media too often accept as fact, aiding only those who profit from public hysteria.

Examples of highly counterproductive stories include one claiming that hundreds of thousands of rabid bats were attacking and harassing the citizens of a Texas town, despite the fact that there was neither evidence of an outbreak nor a single instance of a bat attack. In another case, a Missouri animal control administrator claimed that "bats really do like to attack dogs and cats" and warned people to go indoors if they saw bats. An Alabama rabies inspector claimed that bats can transmit rabies to people "by simply breathing on the victim," and a Washington, D.C., newspaper warned of an impending migratory invasion of 2 million bats, from which rabid ones could be expected to drop on people. Last but not least, an article in a national women's magazine claimed that a family was trapped in their home for three days while bats attacked the windows and doors. The following excerpt is from Dr. Constantine's letter to the editor responsible for that article: "*The Nightmare House* describes the kind of hysteria that can be caused by this and similarly misleading articles. . . . Your article will aid those seeking profit in their nationwide drive to create hysteria and demand for relaxation of government restriction of toxicants for bat control, a practice that guarantees them a steady income, because the poisoned bats are soon replaced by other bats."

Dr. Constantine further notes that overreaction often consists of deliberate efforts to seek out and destroy bats, "resulting in scattering disabled bats, sometimes throughout an entire town, increasing some tenfold the numbers of persons and animals bitten as they handle the downed bats."

*A bat that suddenly appears in your home is probably a lost youngster, primarily concerned with making a safe escape. Mexican free-tailed bats (*Tadarida brasiliensis) *are common visitors in southern and western states.*

Dealing with Unexpected Visitors

PANIC AVOIDANCE

The most serious problems arising from the sudden appearance of a bat are those created by panicked responses. Bats that appear in people's homes are often lost youngsters who are at least as afraid of humans as we are of them. Their only interest is in a safe escape.

In a lifetime of studying bats, I have caught and handled many thousands of individual bats, and never once have I been attacked by one — no matter how long I chased it! Although a bat flying around a room often appears to be attacking, anyone who simply stands still for a moment will quickly learn better. To understand the underlying reason for the bat's apparent swoops at your head, just put yourself in the same situation and imagine that you are the pilot of a small airplane. You cross the room, having to make a U-turn each time you come to a corner. When you make the turn you must virtually stop, causing a stall; and, as any pilot knows, you must quickly swoop downward to regain flight speed and control. The bottom of the swoop will occur near the middle of the room, where observers are most likely to be standing. This, of course, gives the false impression that the bat is attacking, and given most people's preconceived ideas of bats as vicious, they run before discovering that the bat would have steered around them if they had just stood still.

A sudden exit from the house is perhaps the worst possible action. By the time help can be found, the bat likely will have wandered into another part of the house and gone to sleep. It then becomes nearly impossible to find. Alternatively, it may have found its own way out, but in either case, people will have to live with the fear of its reappearance for a week or more.

REMOVAL

Most bats will be active, probably flying, when found, but some may be roosting and asleep. Especially during cool weather, a few will be torpid. Torpor is a state of greatly reduced activity and metabolism that results from a lowering of body temperature. These bats can be so lethargic as to appear sick or even dead. As they arouse, they may bare their teeth and squeak or hiss loudly, leading people to think they are vicious. In reality, they are simply trying to ward off possible attack during a period of relative helplessness. They should not be handled without leather work gloves, because they are more likely than usual to bite in self-defense if touched at such times.

An arousing bat often is incapable of flight for several minutes to an hour. It must first warm itself by shivering; the lower the bat's body temperature, the longer it takes to warm itself. In the meantime, it can be gently scraped into a can or box, allowed to arouse in a covered container in a warm place, and released outside when fully awake. Big brown bats, the ones most often found in such a state, can be released into temperatures as low as 25°F without harm, preferably at dusk.

A bat found flying around in a home should be kept in sight while all doors leading to other parts of the house are closed, thereby isolating it in a single room. Then, if possible, windows or doors to the outside should be opened, so the bat can leave on its own. You need not turn the lights off to be successful.

If you prefer being a bit more decisive, there are more direct approaches to hastening the bat's exit. If a small mesh net (such as a butterfly net) is available, swing it from behind the bat to avoid detection. Otherwise, wait until

If a bat strays into your living quarters and you can't easily chase it out an open window or door, then you may wish to capture it in an old coffee can or similar container. Once the bat has landed, approach it slowly to avoid frightening it into flight. Slip the container over the bat and use a piece of cardboard to close the opening. The bat can be released outside without harm.

the bat lands, and approach it slowly to avoid frightening it back into flight. Then clamp a small box or coffee can over it, and slide a piece of cardboard under the container to trap the bat inside.

Another approach requires a small mailing tube, or one left from a roll of paper towels. Seal one end, and leave the other open. Slowly move the tube into a horizontal position next to the bat, and it often will crawl inside in an attempt to hide. You also can catch it in a towel or gloved hands. It may bite in self-defense when grabbed, but not through leather work gloves.

Release the bat outdoors, and you can be confident that it is unlikely to be found indoors again. Bats have good memories and don't like to repeat close calls with giants. Of course, others may appear if you do not find out how that bat entered and prevent further access.

PREVENTING OTHER VISITS

Bats that suddenly appear in people's living quarters have usually entered through rather predictable routes. The most obvious are open doors and windows; two other common routes are ungrated chimneys and loose-fitting screen doors. A piece of half-inch mesh hardware cloth over the top of the chimney or a tighter fitting screen door will do the trick. If there is a stairwell leading to an attic, check to see if a space exists at the bottom of the door. Young bats are less skilled fliers and sometimes get trapped in stairwells where they end up crawling under the door. A draft guard will solve the problem.

If none of the previous solutions fit your situation or if problems persist after the more obvious routes have been closed, then conduct a room-by-room search for less conspicuous entry points. Any hole more than a half inch in diameter or any crack of at least a quarter of an inch by an inch and a half or more should be closed, especially those leading to outer walls or an attic. Air intakes may need a screen covering, and open spaces around plumbing can be closed by simply stuffing them with steel wool, an approach that will also exclude mice. Even duct tape can be used to exclude bats, because unlike rodents, bats do not chew holes in walls, nor do they gnaw electrical insulation.

There are a few homes of such construction or disrepair that it is not economically feasible or otherwise practical to exclude bats from outer walls, roofs, or attics, but even under these circumstances it should be possible to exclude bats from the living quarters.

Evicting Unwelcome Tenants

NUISANCE PROBLEMS

Large numbers of bats living in an attic or wall space can be a nuisance. Fortunately, most colonies are small, often remaining unnoticed for many years. When discovery of a small colony leads to panic, a little education may be the only action needed. Where guano accumulations or noises from larger groups require a solution, eviction and exclusion are the only safe, permanent remedies.

REPELLENTS

Unfortunately, no ultrasonic or chemical repellents appear to be even moderately effective in eliminating bats from their day roosts in buildings. Ultrasonic devices thus far tested are highly ineffective, and some may endanger people or even attract bats. Chemical repellents, such as moth balls, are mostly effective in generating repeat business for pest control companies and may be hazardous to the health of humans when used in quantities sufficient to drive bats out. They soon evaporate and the bats return.

Similarly, burning sulfur candles can force bats to exit an attic temporarily, but it will not provide a long-term solution and must be done with great caution to avoid fire hazards. Other remedies include adding lights to an attic or increasing ventilation, though these are seldom more than partially effective.

Aerosol dog and cat repellents may discourage bats from using a particular night roosting spot, such as above a porch, for periods of up to several months and are quite useful for these limited situations. They can be sprayed onto roosting site surfaces, but never should be applied while bats are present. Aside from being inhumane, spraying the bats may cause them to dart accidentally into the face of their attacker in an attempt to escape. They also may become ill or grounded, hence increasing the probability of contact with people or pets.

EXCLUSION

Any bat colony large enough to be a real nuisance contains sufficient individuals to easily indicate the point of entry to their roosting place. When they emerge at dusk to feed, watch the building to see where they leave. Closer inspection during the day should reveal the holes or cracks through which they are exiting. Often, these will be under the eaves, behind a chimney or loose board, beneath a roof's ridge cap, or inside an opening made by squirrels or birds. Exact locations may be further identified by stains caused by body oils or droppings. Once exits have been located, the bats can be excluded. This should not be done when flightless young may be present (usually in June or July). Besides being an unnecessary cruelty, excluding the parents will starve the young and create an odor problem.

In the United States most bats leave their roosts in buildings in the fall, permitting exclusion during their winter absence. When this is not the case, or when one does not wish to wait that long, there is a relatively simple exclusion technique using half-inch polypropylene bird netting. Hang the netting during the day, directly above exits, using duct tape or staples. The netting should be attached several inches above the bats' exit holes, extending at least 1 foot to each side and below. The sides may be attached to the building, but the bottom must be allowed to hang free, permitting the bats passage to the outside. They have no trouble dropping down to leave, but when they attempt

Bat colonies living in buildings often enter through predictable routes; any space as large as a quarter of an inch wide by an inch and a half or more long is a possibility. Close inspection of suspected entry points usually will reveal brown stains from body oils where the bats squeeze in and out and possibly a few mouselike droppings adhering to the building just below.

To exclude bats from a building use bird netting. Hang it over entry points so that it extends at least two feet below and to each side, the bottom edge being allowed to hang loosely from one to several inches away from the side of the building. This allows emerging bats to crawl under and out, but returning bats are unable to find their way in. The netting is normally used to protect fruit trees from birds, and it can be purchased from garden centers and some hardware stores.

to fly straight in upon their return, the netting acts as a one-way exclusion valve until repairs can be made. Allow two to three nights to ensure that no bats are trapped inside. The bats' entry holes can then be closed at one's convenience. The netting, mostly used to protect fruit trees from birds, is inexpensive. It should be available in a local hardware or garden store.

Exclusion of bats from Spanish or concrete tile roofs also can be achieved with the use of bird netting, but preventing their return is complicated by the many potential points of entry under open-ended tiles along the roof margins and sometimes along ridges. The simplest solution is to install rain gutters along the edges on all sides of the building. Open ends of tile along ridges can be filled with cement (to within 6 inches of the outer openings), though this is usually unnecessary. The gutters must be completely flush against the surfaces to which they are attached, and the upper edges must be even with the lower edges of tiles, extending outward about 8 inches. Downspouts should be left open-ended and unattached to vertical drains until the bats are no longer present. This prevents clogging by bats that might fall in. Rain gutters can be installed without prior exclusion, since the bats remain able to leave. They do not return, because they apparently dislike climbing over the slick metal rain gutters. Plugging ridge openings, if necessary, should be done only after exclusion.

POISONS

Scientific and public health literature documents that poisons used against bats are ineffective in eliminating bats from buildings and that they can create problems far worse than any they were intended to solve. They may even reduce bats' natural resistance to viral infection, increasing the odds of their contracting rabies. Some of these poisons pose potentially serious health hazards to people. They all can greatly increase contact between bats, people, and pets, because sick and dying bats fall to the ground where they may remain active for days.

An anticoagulant tracking powder, chlorophacinone (Rozol), is one of the poisons most widely used against bats in the United States, and it provides an excellent example of why toxicants should not be used in their control. It is a powerful anticoagulant that takes years to degrade in buildings, and animal tests indicate that it is greater than 80 times more toxic than a related anticoagulant known to cause serious birth defects in human infants whose mothers came into contact with it during pregnancy. The poison can be absorbed directly through human skin, and it has caused neurologic and cardiopulmonary injury and even death in lab animals before clinical signs could be detected.

For control of bats, chlorophacinone is blown into attics and wall spaces, up to 18 pounds at a time. In a U.S. Environmental Protection Agency hearing in Minneapolis the judge noted that as it "is used to exterminate bats in an attic, the powder would be blown around throughout the living spaces of the house due to the downward drift of air currents." He concluded that each use of chlorophacinone against bats had "presented a serious hazard of harm to people and the environment."

Dr. Stephen Frantz, a rodent and bat specialist for the Wadsworth Center for Laboratories and Research at the New York Department of Health, recently investigated homes whose attics had been treated in bat control and found that chlorophacinone dust does spread to human living quarters. He agrees that this is a potentially widespread and serious hazard in states where the compound has been used against bats.

Dr. Denny Constantine provides an example illustrating the danger to humans. He was contacted by the father of a three-year-old Minnesota child who had been ill since chlorophacinone was blown into the attic above her room some two and a half years previously (followed by a second application a year later). Overt symptoms were those of a chronic pneumonia, and the child's lungs were extensively scarred before the real problem could be identified. In fact, neither the child's parents nor the family physician suspected she was being poisoned until local publicity about the danger of chlorophacinone use in bat control prompted the father to call Dr. Constantine for advice.

A pest control operator had frightened the family into using the chemical, despite the fact that no bats could be found in the attic. Evidently a bat had flown into the house through an open window. At last report, the family had moved out of their home and were trying to remove the poison, which had infiltrated the insulation among other things.

For the above reasons, the U.S. government no longer registers any chemicals as safe for bat control and, in fact, has strongly advised against such use. Poisoning of bats is now illegal in many states. Nevertheless, much poisoning continues illegally, and more than 15 states still permit legal use of toxicants, including chlorophacinone, against bats. This poses potentially serious public health hazards, even for people who may unknowingly purchase treated homes years later. All suspected use of poisons against bats should be reported to appropriate

Dr. Stephen Frantz, a rodent and bat specialist with the New York Department of Health, inspects a home for chlorophacinone (Rozol) contamination. This potent anticoagulant can be absorbed directly through human skin, so he wears an elaborate protective suit, illustrating the risk to unsuspecting home owners. (Photograph by Stephen C. Frantz.)

state authorities, and homes treated in the past should be evaluated for continuing hazards.

FINDING AN HONEST, WELL-INFORMED PEST CONTROL COMPANY

To find a reliable pest control company, call several, briefly describe your problem, and ask their recommendations. Beware of scare tactics; remember that even sick bats rarely attack people or pets. They don't multiply like rabbits, and they won't suddenly show up in droves because of scent from others. Such claims indicate a preoccupation with sales, not with helping the customer. Be especially careful to avoid those companies that recommend the use of poisons. They often charge hundreds of dollars to poison bats and then attempt to convince the customer of their honesty by offering a one-year guarantee. The profit margin is so high that they can easily afford to return when the bats do. You are likely to end up with a poisoned home in addition to still having bats!

Permanent physical exclusion is a mandatory part of any bat control job, and when this is done properly poisons are unnecessary. The use of poisons simply provides an excuse for charging more. Also, beware of claimed needs to spray for parasites. These are seldom a problem and will die anyway without their hosts. Spraying for parasites may actually drive them into human living quarters, creating a situation that would not have existed if they had simply been left alone.

There are honest pest control companies, and some are quite knowledgeable about bats and proper exclusion techniques. If you cannot find one, you may want to simply hire a carpenter and explain what needs to be done. It's really not that difficult in most cases.

These pallid bats are resting at a night roost under the eaves of an old building in western Texas.

Living in Harmony

VALUED NEIGHBORS

Bats are important indicators of a healthy environment, and they should be a welcome part of our neighborhoods. Like canaries in a mine, they serve as early warning systems for dangerously high pesticide and pollution levels. The occasional nuisance situation can be remedied, often easily, without having to fear or declare war on bats. Their presence is clearly beneficial — they will leave you alone, but mosquitoes won't!

As more people learn not to fear bats, an increasingly frequent question is, "Do they really eat mosquitoes?" The answer is an unequivocal yes, and at that task they probably have a much greater impact than either the famed purple martins or electric bug zappers. Relatively few mosquitoes are attracted to bug zappers, and you may have noticed that martins go to sleep at about the time that mosquitoes are waking up. Most bats in the United States include some mosquitoes in their diets, and the smaller species consume many. In a lab experiment, mouse-eared bats released into a room full of flying mosquitoes caught up to 600 each in an hour. Bats also eat numerous agricultural pests, including corn borers, grain and cutworm moths, potato beetles, and grasshoppers. One study showed that corn borer damage to a test plot could be reduced by more than half, just by broadcasting batlike ultrasounds in the vicinity. Many insects actually listen for bats and veer away when a bat is heard.

Residents of the famed Chautauqua summer resort in New York do not use pesticides. For more than 50 years they have encouraged bats to live there as an alternative to chemical forms of mosquito control, and they report great success. Recent restoration efforts have excluded some bats, and the residents, who greatly value bats, are now seeking advice on how to rebuild their bat population.

Several years ago I was invited there to lecture, with one purpose being to educate younger generations regarding the importance of continued bat protection. My hosts credited bats for the town's scarcity of mosquitoes, and I was, of course, curious to see for myself. For three summer evenings I walked Chautauqua's streets and enjoyed its outdoor amphitheaters; sure enough, I wasn't bitten a single time. At dusk thousands of bats could be seen hunting, more than I have seen in any other town in eastern North America. The only insect I noticed was caught by a bat within seconds.

Some might argue that such effective biological control is impossible, since every predator must leave something for the future, but Chautauqua's bats don't spend the whole evening feeding near their roosts. Undoubtedly, they eat what is close at hand first and then move out into surrounding areas where they have a far less noticeable impact. No one has scientifically investigated the validity of the Chautauquans' claims, but the circumstances certainly seem to support their faith in bats.

EXTENDING AN INVITATION

If you would like to invite bats to your yard, you can do so by putting up a bat house. Bat houses have been used for more than 60 years in Europe, but they only recently have become popular in the United States and Canada. Surprisingly little research has been done to determine bat roosting preferences, but we do know that there are several factors crucial to the success of bat houses. These include daily temperature profile (determined by house size,

Bat houses should be positioned at least 10 to 15 feet or more off the ground, facing east or southeast to catch the morning sun. The entry should be free of such obstructions as branches.

shape, insulation, and placement), the size and shape of internal roosting spaces, roughness of the surfaces to which the bats must cling, and the distances to drinking and feeding areas.

Mark Hodgkins recently studied bat nursery roosts in manmade structures in the northwestern United States and found that they were all located within roughly a thousand feet of a river, lake, or pond. He also found significant preferences for particular roost sizes, shapes, and temperature profiles. Many roosts, especially small ones, cooled so much at night that they fell below the optimum temperature range for their nursery colonies. It was probably for this reason that orientation to the sun was found to be important. Roosts facing east and southeast were optimally oriented to the morning sun, heating more quickly and having a higher daily heat gain.

On the basis of these findings, Hodgkins designed two kinds of artificial bat houses, one for small insectivorous bats, such as mouse-eared bats, and the other for their larger counterparts, the big brown and pallid bats. His bat houses were similar to an earlier design, known as the "Missouri-style" bat house, except that they were smaller, for convenience of construction, and better accommodated the bats' observed preferences for roosting crevice depths and widths. A much smaller bat house of European design has been successful in some areas and occasionally has attracted as many as 30 bats. However, these houses are too small to provide temperature stability, and they do not offer a variety of crevice widths to accommodate different species. It seems likely that they are used primarily when better alternatives are unavailable. Sometimes these have solid bottoms, making them more likely to be taken over

A Missouri-style bat house at the Lindbergh Interpretive Center in Little Falls, Minnesota. This house was first occupied a little more than a year after it was built, and it now contains a colony of little brown bats that has doubled in size each year for the past three years. Eleven similar houses are now used in other Minnesota parks. One house is capable of sheltering hundreds of bats. (Photograph by Earl Johnson.)

by wrens, mice, squirrels, or other unwanted animals.

The Missouri-style bat house is large enough to shelter hundreds of bats. It is approximately 7½ feet long, 4 feet wide, and 2½ feet tall and is open at the bottom for entry. The main bat roosting areas consist of variably spaced (¾ inch, 1 inch, 1¼ inch), wooden partitions inside two 6 × 1 × 1 foot compartments joined side by side. Spaces at the ends permit bats to enter the "attic" above the compartments, but most seem to prefer the crevices. The greatest advantage of the attic is probably its influence in stabilizing daily temperature fluctuations in the roost. As the name implies, the first one was built in Missouri, and the success of that one led to the construction of several more in Minnesota. Of the first two placed in Minnesota parks, one was occupied within a year, and the second after a year and a half. Their little brown bat occupants apparently preferred the ¾-inch crevices. The most carefully monitored house was initially occupied by 15 bats. This number increased to 40 the second year and to more than 85 the third. Its population is still growing, and 10 additional Missouri-style bat houses recently have been built for other Minnesota parks.

In response to public interest in bat houses, Bat Conservation International (BCI), a nonprofit organization dedicated to bat conservation, bat research, and public education, has designed a version that is a compromise between the large complex types and the smallest simple ones. The BCI design is relatively easy to build, but still incorporates several of the crevice widths and depths suggested by Hodgkins, to accommodate large and small species. Its 27-inch height and small attic help to provide more stable temperatures over a greater range.

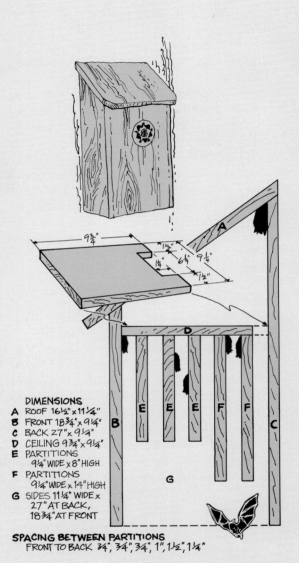

DIMENSIONS
A ROOF 16½" x 11¼"
B FRONT 18¾" x 9¼"
C BACK 27" x 9¼"
D CEILING 9¾" x 9¼"
E PARTITIONS
   9¼" WIDE x 8" HIGH
F PARTITIONS
   9¼" WIDE x 14" HIGH
G SIDES 11¼" WIDE x
   27" AT BACK,
   18¾" AT FRONT

SPACING BETWEEN PARTITIONS
FRONT TO BACK ¾", ¾", ¾", 1", 1½", 1¼"

A bat house designed by Bat Conservation International combines relative ease of construction with the varied crevice sizes most often used by American bats and temperature buffering features. Western red cedar is recommended for its ability to withstand outdoor exposure, though many other woods are suitable. Six feet of 1 x 12-inch board and 10 feet of 1 x 10-inch board are sufficient for construction. (Actual board sizes normally are about ¾ x 9¼ inches and ¾ x 11¼ inches.) Overall dimensions may be varied to allow for slight differences in board widths or personal preferences, but spacing between partitions should remain approximately the same. Use rough lumber and turn the rough sides of the roof, front, back, and sides inward. The rough side of the ceiling should face down. Cut 1/16-inch horizontal grooves at ½-inch intervals on the smooth sides of all partitions. This will enable bats to climb and roost. Apply a bead of silicone caulk along each exterior joint to prevent heat loss. The estimated cost of materials is less than $20, and a single house may be occupied by a hundred or more bats.

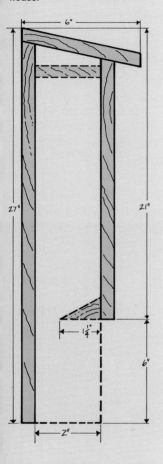

This and a slightly smaller version of this bat house can be purchased ready-made from BCI.

All inner surfaces of bat houses, regardless of the kind built, must be rough or horizontally grooved so that bats can get a firm foothold. Rough-sided lumber is adequate but usually planed on one side, requiring the cutting of 1/16-inch horizontal grooves into the surface of the smooth side of each roosting partition at about 1/2-inch intervals. For the roof, front, back, and sides the planed surface can be turned to the outside. When putting a house together, the contact points between the sides, front, back, and roof should be carefully caulked to eliminate air circulation except from the open bottom. This permits the bat's body heat to be trapped, likely increasing the probability of occupancy.

In constructing any bat house, no chemically treated woods should be used. Some lumber is impregnated with wood preservatives or insecticides that could harm bats.

Even without a bat house, you may provide a roost for a few bats simply by using an 18-inch-wide piece of tar paper or similar material. Wrap and staple it completely around a tree trunk so that it is tight at the top and flares out about 2 inches at the bottom. This permits bats to select shady or sunny sides as their temperature needs change over the day and season.

Roost requirements vary widely according to climate, species, and social group. For example, nursery colonies of larger species, such as big brown and pallid bats, like roost temperatures in the 80°–90°F (27°–32°C) range, while those of smaller species, such as mouse-eared and free-tailed bats, seem to prefer 90°–110°F (32°–43°C). Some live in roosts where temperatures reach as high as 120°F (49°C). Bachelor groups tend to choose cooler locations. Even in nature, few roosts are perfect. Given the divergent preferences among sexes and species, houses with a variety of temperature profiles all have at least some chance of success. To provide a wider range of temperatures, Europeans sometimes mount their houses on trees in sets of four, with each facing a different direction.

Geographic variation in summer temperatures must be given serious consideration in selecting sites for bat houses. With increasing latitude, altitude, or both, average temperatures are lower, and bat houses for nursery colonies must be oriented for maximum sunlight, especially early morning sunlight. They may also need tar paper or dark-colored shingles on the upper portion of the box to increase heat absorption. Paint should be avoided, because it can have a repellent effect. At one site in a cool climate, bats ignored an artificial roost until a thermostat-controlled heating unit was supplied.

In exceptionally hot climates, bat houses may require shade. A maximum-minimum thermometer can be used to test the interior temperatures of a house in several locations before choosing a permanent site, though this is probably not necessary. Tall houses may be most successful because they provide better internal temperature gradients, permitting bats to move up and down inside to adjust for temperature variations over the day or season.

Other considerations are height above the ground, ease of access, and wind protection. Houses have been occupied at heights as low as 6 feet, but 10–15 feet is much better. Some bats, especially free-tailed bats, prefer heights of 20–40 feet or more. Never place a house where the approach is obstructed, such as by tree limbs or vegetation. If possible, choose a site that is relatively protected from prevailing winds.

Experience thus far indicates that, though a few houses have been used on the first night, most are not used for at least a year. As with bird houses, some proportion may never be occupied, though in my personal experience, most have been used. Those attached to the side of a building have had the most success, perhaps because of added temperature stability. Two houses put up by a friend who seemed to have done almost everything wrong were occupied a year later. In an instance in which two houses were mounted only a few feet apart, one was used by 30 bats, while the other was ignored. In another case, a bat house was attached to the side of a building, leaving a small space between the house and the building. Bats never moved into the house, but lived in the gap! In at least one instance a bat house was ignored even though it was conveniently situated near natural roosts from which bats were excluded. Such examples illustrate that we still have a lot to learn about attracting bats.

You can assist greatly with bat conservation efforts by performing your own bat house experiments and reporting the results, both successful and unsuccessful, to Bat Conservation International (see For Additional Information, page viii). Many bats are losing their natural roosts, and they need homes, but we must learn much more about their requirements before we can adequately provide for them.

ADDITIONAL NEEDS

Unfortunately, helping bats means more than just building bat houses. It was once believed that pesticides were the primary cause of bat decline. Carelessly used pesticides do kill bats, as is well documented, and bats are far more easily killed by pesticides and pollution than

are mosquitoes. However, we now recognize that direct human persecution and loss of roost sites often threaten them even more.

Most species that will live in bat houses also require very specific winter quarters in caves. It is no coincidence that all bats federally listed as endangered in the continental United States spend at least half of their lives in caves. Vastly increased interest in cave exploration over the past 20 years is believed to be one of the most important causes of bat decline. Some species live in caves year-round and are especially threatened. Others require caves only for hibernation, but even these are highly vulnerable. Human disturbance has eliminated bats from hibernating sites in many areas. Summer disturbances often cause abandonment of nursery roosts and the death of baby bats.

Professional cave explorers, better known as speleologists, are becoming increasingly involved in helping to protect sites that are essential to bats. However, many of the people who explore caves are amateurs who do not appreciate the disasters that can be caused by seemingly harmless disturbance. Each winter intrusion causes hibernating bats to arouse, wasting, on the average 10 to 30 days' worth of fat reserves. Since the bats are insectivorous, they cannot feed during the winter, and mass starvation can result before energy reserves can be replenished in the spring. These unnecessary intrusions continue to kill countless thousands of bats each year, often accounting for their decline over thousands of square miles around a single disturbed cave.

Few caves are essential to bats year-round, and less than 5 percent of temperate-zone caves are suitable for colonies at any time. Most of the relatively few used are occupied only in

These endangered gray bats (Myotis grisescens) are hibernating in a Tennessee cave. Nearly all gray bats must overwinter in just nine caves, making them extremely vulnerable. Loss of cave roosts through human disturbance and vandalism is believed to be the primary cause for the alarming 80 percent-plus decline of gray bats.

This hibernating eastern pipistrelle (Pipistrellus subflavus) has droplets of condensed moisture on its fur, indicating that its body temperature has dropped to that of the cave. These bats hibernate individually and are the species most often encountered by cave explorers.

winter for hibernation or in summer as nursery sites, and they can be explored without harm to bats by simply timing trips to coincide with periods when the bats are absent. If bats are accidentally encountered, they should not be disturbed.

Additional losses have resulted from poorly planned guano extraction, careless research, and overcollecting of bats. Guano, which is sometimes removed for fertilizer, should not be removed by novices or when bats are present, and researchers should carefully plan their studies in a manner that does not harm bat populations. Aided by modern technology, such as nighttime viewing scopes and ultrasonic detectors, many previously impossible behavioral and ecological studies of bats are now feasible, and they can be extremely fascinating as well as essential to management and conservation planning.

CONSERVATION

The list of bat contributions to the health and welfare of humans is very long. Yet, despite their many demonstrated values, bats remain among the most intensely feared, relentlessly persecuted, even scientifically neglected animals on earth. Unfortunately, they are exceptionally vulnerable to extinction, typically rearing only one young per year and forming the largest, most vulnerable aggregations of any warm-blooded animal. Millions have been burned, poisoned, or dynamited in single acts. Worldwide, bats are declining at alarming rates, needless victims of continued human misunderstanding.

In 1963, the world's largest known bat colony — close to 30 million Mexican free-tails — lived in Eagle Creek Cave, Arizona. However, in just six years their numbers were reduced to a mere

30,000 — a 99.9 percent decline! No one documented exactly what happened, but the hillside in front of the cave is still littered with shotgun and rifle casings. The loss of bats at Eagle Creek Cave leaves more than 350,000 pounds of insects uneaten nightly, inexorably upsetting nature's balance. Such losses leave us increasingly dependent on pesticides that already threaten many aspects of our lives.

Unfortunately, such senseless acts of destruction are still common. In the United States, six species of bats have already required federal listing as endangered, and many more may have to be included if present trends are not reversed. Major population losses are well documented on all continents, and several island species, especially flying foxes, have recently become extinct without even being declared endangered. It is frightening to consider that many of the species needed in large numbers to maintain the balance of nature are, instead, now at such low population levels that they are virtually irrelevant biologically. Bat Conservation International was founded in the hope that when the shrouds of myth and superstition are stripped away, bats will be appreciated as fascinating and likable animals. Even more important, we need bats whether we like them or not; their loss poses serious, potentially irreversible consequences to the environment that we all must share.

The little brown bat is one of
America's most abundant and
widespread species.

Distribution of the mouse-eared
bat (Myotis lucifugus).

Getting to Know Your Neighbors

The bats most often encountered in American homes and yards are conveniently divisible into two groups: those that commonly live in buildings and those that live only in trees. (For illustrated descriptions of the various species' characteristics, see chapter 8.) Surprisingly, even among species most often seen, few have been studied more than superficially. The following accounts summarize current knowledge.

COMMON HOUSE-DWELLERS

Mouse-Eared Bats (*Myotis*)

Distribution   Worldwide there are close to 100 species of mouse-eared bats, all belonging to the genus *Myotis*. Only 15 of these occur in North America north of Mexico; most are so rare or secretive that they are seldom encountered. The little brown bat (*Myotis lucifugus*), a species frequently found in buildings, is the most common mouse-eared bat in Canada and the northern two-thirds of the United States. In other areas a variety of mouse-eared bats with generally similar behavior and appearance may be encountered in buildings, though they usually have been far less studied.

Recognition   American species range in color from brown or russet to gray, and they lack conspicuous markings, except for a few species that have a distinctive black facial mask. All are small with wingspans ranging from 222 mm to 315 mm and forearms from 29 mm to 47 mm. Both little brown and big brown (*Eptesicus fuscus*) bats are often found in buildings, and although they look very similar in many respects, the latter is much larger.

Behavior   Mouse-eared bats occupy a wide variety of summer roosts, including caves, abandoned mines, buildings, tree hollows, cliff faces, cavities beneath large rocks, and even animal burrows. Some have rather narrow requirements, utilizing only one or two kinds of summer roosts; others are much less selective. Most spend the winter hibernating in caves or mines.

Of the mouse-eared bats, the little brown bat is one of the most common and best known to science. In areas where it lives, it is the most likely mouse-eared bat to be found near people's homes, and it often shares its roosts with the big brown bat. Typically, little brown bats live in buildings near a river, marsh, or lake over which they feed on aquatic insects, such as mosquitoes, sometimes catching as many as 600 in an hour.

Little brown bats mate in the fall just before they enter hibernation. Sperm remain dormant in the females until the bats arouse the following spring, at which time ovulation and fertilization occur. Young, usually one per female, are born and reared in June and July. They grow rapidly and learn to fly in about three weeks. Nursery colonies often include 300–800 individuals; a few may contain thousands. They select roosting sites with high, stable temperatures, which explains why they favor attics. They are very heat tolerant, and body temperatures as high as 129°F (54°C) have been reported. Bachelor groups tend to be much smaller and to prefer cooler roosting places.

Summer roosts are abandoned in August or September, and some colonies travel up to 200 miles or more to reach the nearest suitable cave or mine for hibernation. They remain there for the next six to eight months, during which they must survive solely on the fat that they were able to store in the last few weeks of summer. *Importance to Humans* Mouse-eared bats are highly beneficial. A colony of 500, when feeding on mosquitoes, can easily catch a quarter of a million or more in a single hour. However, because of the large size of the nursery colonies of some species that roost in buildings, they are among the most often involved in nuisance complaints in America. Conversely, they are rarely implicated in public health problems.

The Big Brown Bat (*Eptesicus fuscus*)

Distribution   The big brown bat is one of the most widely distributed of American bats, ranging from Canada to northern South America and the Caribbean Islands.

Recognition   This is a large brown to copper-colored bat without distinctive markings. It has a wingspan of 325–350 mm, a forearm length of 42–51 mm, and is most often confused with the much smaller mouse-eared and evening bats.

Behavior   Big brown bats typically form colonies in buildings, often behind chimneys, in wall spaces, or under eaves. They also live in tree hollows and beneath loose bark. This species is less tolerant of high temperatures than the mouse-eared bats, usually relocating if temperatures exceed 95°F (35°C). Nursery colonies normally include from 20 to 300 individuals. Bachelors often roost in smaller groups or alone.

Big brown bats feed on a wide variety of insects, but appear to prefer beetles. They hunt in meadows, among scattered trees in pastures, along tree-lined village streets, or even around lights above city traffic.

They are extremely hardy and are capable of surviving subfreezing body temperatures. For this reason, the big brown bat is the only North American species that commonly overwinters in walls or attics as far north as Canada. When caves or mines are available for hibernation, these bats may travel up to 150 miles to reach

them. Bats that hibernate in buildings often must move from one roost to another during weather extremes and, at such times, may be encountered by people. Even in the northern United States, they frequently remain active until November or December, and apparently healthy individuals have been caught while flying in blizzard conditions.

Big brown bats mate during periods of activity in fall and winter, and females store sperm until spring. They become pregnant on resumption of activity in March or April. One to two young are born in late May or early June and are able to fly within a month.

Importance to Humans   Of all the North American species, this is the one most closely associated with humans because of its year-round use

Distribution of the big brown bat (Eptesicus fuscus).

The big brown bat is found throughout most of the United States and Canada. It feeds principally on beetles.

of buildings. Not surprisingly, it also is the species most often implicated in public health problems. This is owed, in part, to its larger size and ability to bite when carelessly handled. Though not an important consumer of mosquitoes, it does eat large quantities of other insects. On balance, it is highly beneficial and poses very little threat if simply left alone.

The Evening Bat (*Nycticeius humeralis*)

Distribution   East of the Appalachians, the evening bat ranges from southern Pennsylvania to Florida; west of these mountains, it occurs north to extreme southern Michigan, west to southeastern Nebraska, and south through East and South Texas. It is one of the most abundant bats around towns in the southern coastal states.

Recognition   Evening bats are small, brown, and lacking in distinctive characteristics. Their wingspan is 260–280 mm, and their forearm length is 33–39 mm. Evening bats have a tragus (see key in next chapter), which is short, curved, and rounded, unlike the long, straight, and pointed tragus typical of mouse-eared bats.

Behavior   Small colonies of evening bats have been found behind loose bark, in hollow trees, in Spanish moss, and beneath dead palm fronds. Nursery groups in buildings may include several hundred individuals.

The enlarged testes of males during the fall suggest mating at that time; most aspects of their reproductive behavior are poorly known. Mothers give birth to a single young that grows rapidly and is capable of first flight within three weeks or less.

Little is known of their feeding behavior or seasonal movements. Northern populations of evening bats accumulate large fat deposits in the fall and then simply disappear. They do not hibernate in local caves, and no one has documented exactly where they go. A few recaptures of banded individuals demonstrate that at least some move south during the fall, including one movement of 325 miles. Recent reports from Florida indicate greatly increased numbers roosting beneath palm fronds there in winter, suggesting likely migration to overwinter in milder southern climates. Southern populations appear to be active most of the year.

Distribution of the evening bat (Nycticeius humeralis).

Importance to Humans When large nursery colonies occur in buildings they can be a nuisance, but this is relatively rare. The species is seldom implicated in public health problems, and its insectivorous feeding habits are presumed beneficial.

The Pallid Bat (*Antrozous pallidus*)

Distribution   The pallid bat is found from Mexico and the extreme southwestern United States north through Oregon, Washington, and western Canada. A few isolated colonies live in southern Kansas and northern Oklahoma.

Recognition   This is a large pale species, yellowish to cream-colored above and white below. The dorsal fur is lightest at the base and becomes darker at the tips. The pallid bat's ears are its most striking characteristic. They are nearly half as long as the combined length of the bat's head and body, and each ear is more than half as wide as long. These are relatively large bats; the wingspan is 360–390 mm, and the forearm length is 48–60 mm. Big-eared bats (*Plecotus townsendii* and *P. phyllotis*) have narrower ears and dorsal fur that is darker at the base than at the tips. The leaf-nosed bat (*Macrotus californicus*) also has large ears, but it is distinguished by a prominent nose leaf not found on any other big-eared bat living north of Mexico.

Behavior   The pallid bat is abundant in many arid, low-elevation regions but scarce at localities above 6,000 feet. It lives in deep crevices in rock faces, buildings, or bridges and is one of the last to emerge in the evening, usually not until it is quite dark. Pallid bats apparently feed almost entirely on the ground and commonly prey on crickets, grasshoppers, June and ground beetles, and even scorpions.

Segregation between bachelor and nursery colonies is common, though both sexes often mix in the same groups. Most colonies are small, ranging from a dozen to 100 individuals. Pallid bats appear not to make lengthy seasonal migrations, though they divide into smaller, less conspicuous groups in the fall. During the win-

Evening bats are common inhabitants of buildings in much of eastern North America, especially in the Gulf states.

ter they sometimes move deeper into rock crevices but may also hibernate in local caves.

Mating begins in late October and is believed to occur sporadically through at least February. Ovulation and fertilization usually take place in the first two weeks of April, and the young, normally twins, are born in the first half of June. They mature relatively slowly and do not learn to fly until they are five or six weeks old.

Importance to Humans These bats feed on insects that are often a problem for people. When their night roosts are over porches they are sometimes considered a nuisance, but their colonies are usually too small to cause other problems.

Distribution of the pallid bat (Antrozous pallidus).

The Pallid bat (Antrozous pallidus), *unlike most North American bats, seldom catches flying insects. Instead, prey such as this scorpion is captured directly from the ground or from foliage. Their big ears allow for extra sensitive hearing. It is believed that they can detect sounds even as faint as a scorpion's footsteps.*

Free-Tailed Bats (*Tadarida* and *Eumops*)

Distribution   Worldwide there are more than 90 species of free-tailed bats. Most occur in tropical and subtropical climates. The six species that occur in the United States range from Miami north to South Carolina, in all of the Gulf states, in the Midwest north to Nebraska, and throughout the Southwest.

Recognition   Free-tailed bats are easily recognized because at least a third of their tail protrudes beyond the membrane that connects the legs and tail, hence the name *free-tail*. Tails of other American bats are almost entirely enclosed in the tail membrane. Free-tails that live in the United States lack distinctive markings and are gray, brown, or russet. Their ears are large and rounded. The upper lips of members of the genus *Tadarida* are vertically wrinkled, but those of *Eumops* are not. Adult individuals of species in the former genus are smaller than those in the latter.

Behavior   The Mexican free-tailed bat (*T. brasiliensis*) is the only free-tailed species commonly encountered in the United States, and for that reason, it is the only one featured in this discussion. Most Mexican free-tailed bats in the United States live in only about a dozen caves, where they form the largest colonies of any warm-blooded animal. One enormous colony in Texas's Bracken Cave includes more than 20 million individuals. That's approximately 240 metric tons of bats! Evening flights begin as much as two hours before sundown and are among the most spectacular sights in nature. Great undulating columns of emerging bats are visible for up to 2 miles.

These bats consume enormous quantities of insects, mostly moths, some apparently feeding continuously throughout the night. The bats from Bracken Cave consume an estimated quarter of a million pounds of insects nightly. Although the largest groups live in caves, this species also forms sizable colonies in buildings, especially on the West Coast and in the Gulf states from Texas east. The Mexican free-tail is primarily a cave bat in Arizona, New Mexico, Oklahoma, and Texas, using buildings mostly for stopover sites during migration. However, even in these areas colonies containing hundreds and sometimes many thousands of individuals can be found living in buildings or under bridges. More than half a million live under the Congress Avenue bridge in Austin, Texas, making that bat colony the largest urban bat colony in the world. Their dusk departures, especially in July and August, are one of the most impressive urban wildlife spectacles in America.

Most free-tails remain active year-round by migrating south into Mexico and Central America for the winter, often in large flocks. In the southern portion of their range a few over-winter in buildings and survive by undergoing brief periods of torpor, but even in these areas, most appear to leave for warmer climates.

Mating occurs in February and March; ovulation in late March. Each female bears a single young, most within a two-week period in June. The young roost in nearly solid masses at densities sometimes in excess of 500 per square foot, covering hundreds of feet of cave walls. Even so, each mother remembers the location of her own young to within a few inches. As the mothers return from feeding, each baby recognizes its mother's voice, rears up, and calls to aid in its location. Final identification is aided by unique odors. Free-tail pups drink close to 30 percent of their body weight in milk daily and first fly in about five weeks.

Distribution of the Mexican free-tailed bat (Tadarida brasiliensis).

Free-tailed bats are easily recognized by their tails, which protrude well beyond the tail membrane. This one is a Mexican free-tail (Tadarida brasiliensis). *Its long, narrow wings are designed for speed and long-distance travel.*

Importance to Humans   When large colonies of Mexican free-tailed bats occupy buildings they may become quite a nuisance, but they can be excluded. Even in these circumstances, any health threat is infinitely small for people who simply leave the bats alone. Caves occupied by millions of these bats require special precautions before entering. Ammonia fumes from guano decomposition can reach levels lethal to humans, and two researchers are believed to have contracted airborne rabies while working under these unique conditions. There is no evidence to suggest that airborne rabies is a problem in buildings.

Given the incredible numbers of insects eaten, including many pest species, free-tailed bats undoubtedly play a vital role in the checks and balances of nature. Their loss could result in serious environmental consequences.

Mexican free-tailed bats form immense colonies in caves, and their emergence at dusk is among the most spectacular sights in nature. Great columns are often visible for up to 2 miles and may rise to altitudes in excess of 10,000 feet, where tail winds may help the bats achieve speeds of over 60 miles per hour enroute to distant feeding grounds.

COMMON TREE-DWELLERS

The Red Bat (*Lasiurus borealis*)

Distribution   Red bats range from Canada and the United States through most of Latin America. In fact, they are among the most abundant bats in much of Canada and the United States, except for southern Florida and the northwestern United States south through New Mexico.

Recognition   Long angoralike fur and bright color rank red bats among the world's most beautiful mammals. They vary from bright orange to yellowish brown, often with a frosted appearance. Red bats are medium-sized, with a wingspan of 290–332 mm and a forearm length of 35–45 mm. They have long narrow wings, short rounded ears, distinct white markings on shoulders and wrists, and a tail membrane that is entirely furred on the dorsal surface. Unlike most bats, there is fur along the undersurface of the main wing bones.

Red bats are most likely to be confused with the Seminole bat (*Lasiurus seminolus*), a species of nearly identical size and appearance, except for the latter's deep mahogany color. The Seminole bat occurs mostly in the Gulf states and along the southern Atlantic coast. The only other American bat with such characteristic white markings and an entirely furred upper surface of the tail membrane is the hoary bat, which is much larger with distinctive markings and coloration.

Behavior   Red bats characteristically roost in the foliage of deciduous trees and are seldom found far from forests. During the day they hang by one foot, wrapped in their big furry tails, looking like a dead leaf. They live solitary lives and come together only to mate and migrate.

Red bats are among the earliest evening fliers and are veritable speedsters, having been timed at 40 miles per hour in level flight. They normally establish a feeding territory not far from their roosting place and are easily observed flying back and forth in an elliptical flight path. They are most often found along forest edges or around street lamps, where they hunt a wide variety of insects, particularly moths. They sometimes congregate in large numbers around corn cribs to feed on emerging grain moths.

In the milder climates of southern and coastal North America, red bats are often year-

Each Mexican free-tailed bat mother produces only one young per year and amazingly can find her own among the teeming thousands of babies on a cave wall. Young learn to fly in about five weeks.

round residents, but most, especially those living in Canada and the northern United States, undertake long seasonal migrations. At such times, groups of up to 100 have been sighted. Observations suggest that the sexes migrate separately in the spring and occupy different summer and winter ranges in some areas.

As often happens to birds, many run into communications towers and high-rise buildings during migration. Data gathered at such collision sites suggest that bats and birds travel similar migration routes and that there may be a close association between bats and birds that migrate at night. Observations along Lake Michigan in September and October indicate migratory waves utilizing storm fronts to speed them along. Under such circumstances, they might easily achieve speeds of 80 miles an hour. This may account for their collisions with tall obstacles on cloudy nights, since their echolocation reaches only a few feet in front of them.

Red bats are well adapted for surviving low temperatures. Even though most migrate, some overwinter as far north as Ohio, where temperatures often fall below 0°F (−17.8°C). Few have been found in hibernation, but available observations indicate a preference for tree hollows. They respond to subfreezing temperatures by increasing their metabolism just enough to maintain body temperature above the critical lower limit of 23°F (−5°C). Unlike most other hibernating bats, they often arouse and feed, even in January if temperatures rise above 55° or 60°F (13°–16°C). At such times they can be seen feeding in bright sunlight as early as two or three in the afternoon.

Distribution of the red bat (Lasiurus borealis).

A male red bat pauses for the day in a maple tree during its fall migration south from Canada. Males are more brightly colored than females.

Apparently, mating occurs just before or during fall migration, often in September, and may be accomplished during flight. Red bats have been observed copulating in flight, and pairs have been seen falling from the sky while attempting to mate. In one instance, two were seen flying together, with one repeatedly trying to land on the other. It finally succeeded, and the two bats remained joined for about 30 seconds, flying unsteadily with all four wings beating.

Sperm remain dormant in the female over the winter, and fertilization occurs in the spring. The gestation period has been estimated at 80–90 days; young are born from May through early July, progressively later at more northern latitudes. Unlike most bats, mothers frequently give birth to triplets and even quadruplets, though some litters consist of only one or two young. Red bats are exceptionally small and poorly developed at birth, weighing as little as 0.018 ounces. Surprisingly, given their immature condition at birth, they begin flying at three to four weeks and are weaned by the fifth or sixth week.

During the day, each young clutches the mother's perch with one foot, and her body with a wing. They are left at the perch at night when the mother is feeding. When they are very young, she may occasionally move them to a new roost, but they soon become too heavy to be carried. During storms the young cling tightly to their mother. If she loses her grip, their combined weight may cause her to fall to the ground. It is at such times that they are most often found by people. They can be helped by gently moving them to a perch in a tree or bush, but before attempting to help them, it is important to remember that the mother is likely to bite in self-defense and should not be handled with bare hands.

Importance to Humans Red bats almost never enter human habitations and pose extremely little threat to anyone who simply leaves them alone. As illustrated, they are valuable allies in the control of crop pests.

The Hoary Bat (*Lasiurus cinereus*)

Distribution The hoary bat is the most widely distributed bat in North America. It is probably found in all 50 states and is the only native land mammal of Hawaii. It occurs from Iceland and Canada south through Central America to Argentina and Chile, and it has also been reported in Bermuda and the Dominican Republic. The hoary bat is uncommon in the eastern United States but common in the prairie states, the Pacific Northwest, and Canada. It is especially abundant in southern California, Arizona, and New Mexico during migration.

Recognition The hoary bat is one of America's largest, most handsome bats. Its wingspan is 380–410 mm, and its forearm length is 46–58 mm. It is a heavily furred, darkly colored bat. The tips of many of its hairs are white, giving it a frosted, or hoary, appearance. The dorsal surface of its tail membrane is entirely furred, as are the undersides of its major wing bones. White markings on its wrists are conspicuous, and its nearly round ears are contrastingly edged in black. With its unique yellowish or orangish throat collar, this bat is quite distinctive. It is sometimes confused with the silver-haired bat, which is smaller; lacks markings on its ears, wrists, and throat; and is nearly furless under its wings and on the outermost half of the tail membrane.

Behavior Behaviorally, the hoary bat is quite similar to the red bat. It too is solitary except during mating and migration, roosts in foliage, and feeds heavily on moths (though it eats mosquitoes too). It is dissimilar in that, unlike red bats, it often roosts in evergreen rather than deciduous trees. Like red bats, northern populations of hoary bats perform long seasonal migrations, and in cold climates, they also may overwinter in small tree cavities. Some travel

Distribution of the hoary bat
(Lasiurus cinereus).

A hoary bat pauses in a pine
tree in Tennessee. It is one of
America's largest and most
strikingly colored bats.

south into subtropical and possibly even tropical areas.

In most of their summer range and in some areas during spring migration, males and females seem to be geographically segregated. Adult males are rarely found in the eastern and central United States or in the prairie provinces of Canada, which are the areas where most females rear their young. The males are commonly found in the western United States.

Little is known about the hoary bat's mating behavior, and though it may be similar to that of the red bat in many respects, female hoary bats almost invariably give birth to twins. They are born from May to early July, the more northerly the latitude the later the date. Care and growth of the young are similar in hoary and red bats, and in both species, most encounters with people are limited to mothers that fall during storms, unable to carry their tightly clinging offspring. In areas of low disturbance, mother hoary bats are quite loyal to particular roost sites. During three years of investigation in Wisconsin, I observed a mother return to exactly the same place under a blue spruce branch to rear her young each spring.

Importance to Humans   Hoary bats never live in buildings and are rarely encountered except when mothers with young fall during storms or when one is sick or caught by a cat. Under such conditions they are probably the most likely of American bats to bite in self-defense. When grounded they may put up a fierce display, including jumping a foot or more at a time toward their adversary. For this reason, they should not be closely approached when grounded. Roosting hoary bats will simply fly away if disturbed and will only bite if touched; when left alone, they are harmless and beneficial.

Yellow Bats (*Lasiurus ega, L. intermedius*)

Distribution   The southern yellow bat (*L. ega*) is found in the United States only in extreme southern California and extreme southeastern Texas and Arizona; most of these bats live in subtropical and tropical Latin America. The northern yellow bat (*L. intermedius*) ranges from coastal South Carolina and southern Georgia through all but the southern tip of Florida and west through the coastal areas of Alabama, Mississippi, Louisiana, and Texas. Likewise, most of its range is in Central America.

Recognition   As the name implies, these bats are usually yellowish in color, but some are yellowish orange, yellow-brown, or nearly gray. Most of the fur is yellowish, but the tips of its hairs may be gray or brown. The northern yellow bat is slightly larger than its southern counterpart, having a wingspan of 350–390 mm and a forearm of 45–56. The southern yellow bat's wingspan is 335–355 mm and its forearm is 45–48 mm. The ranges of these two species overlap only in the extreme southern tip of Texas. Therefore, with the exception of this small area they can be identified on the basis of locality. Yellow bats are easily distinguished from red bats by the former's tail membranes, which are furred only on the anterior half of the upper surface.

Behavior   The southern yellow bat is not well studied, and it is known in the United States mostly from the Tucson and Phoenix regions. It has been found roosting in a variety of trees, often beneath the dead fronds of palms, and it sometimes hibernates in Washington fan palms.

The northern yellow bat typically roosts singly, sometimes several in one tree, and rears its young in Spanish moss throughout most of its

*Distribution of the yellow bats (*Lasiurus ega *and* L. intermedius). *The southern yellow bat (*Lasiurus ega) *is found mainly in the west, and the northern yellow bat (*L. intermedius) *is found mainly in the Atlantic and Gulf coastal regions. Cross-hatching indicates where species overlap.*

*A southern yellow bat (*Lasiurus ega) *emerges from its day roost under the dead fronds of a palm tree.*

range in the United States. Many are found by professional moss gatherers. In the Rio Grande Valley and farther south it appears to form nursery groups in tall palms.

Although little is known about the southern yellow bat, the northern species forages about 15–25 feet above the ground, often along forest edges and over areas with few shrubs and only scattered trees. Open grassy areas seem to be favored hunting grounds. From June through August, young-of-the-year join their mothers in feeding groups of 20–50 bats. Males appear to feed solitarily except during the winter, when

they too may be found in groups. Yellow bats are insectivorous, but little is known about their specific preferences. Apparently, yellow bats do not migrate, and both species overwinter, at least occasionally, among dead palm fronds.

Very little is known about their mating behavior. On one occasion in November, a copulating pair of northern yellow bats was captured after they fell to the ground. Some females collected in mid-December had already copulated. They give birth anytime from late May through June. The normal litter size is three, but twins and even quadruplets are occasionally recorded.

Importance to Humans Yellow bats do not roost in buildings and therefore are unlikely to be a problem. They are seldom seen except when grounded by illness, and that is probably how the notion arose that there is an unusual prevalence of rabies in this species. As with other bats, if left alone, they are harmless and beneficial.

The Silver-Haired Bat (*Lasionycteris noctivagans*)

Distribution The silver-haired bat is another species that is widely distributed in North America, although it is rare in the Gulf states, Texas, southernmost California, and southwestern Arizona. This bat lives in forested areas, north almost to the tree line in Canada. It is most abundant in the northern Rockies and in parts of New England and New York and is seasonally common (winter and spring) as far south as Arizona and New Mexico in the west and Kentucky and Tennessee in the east.

Recognition Silver-haired bats are usually black or occasionally dark brown. As their name implies, the dorsal fur is frosted with silver tips. The wingspan is 270–310 mm, and the forearm length is 37–44 mm. The upper surface of the tail membrane is furred only on the anterior half. This bat is most often confused with the hoary bat, but the two are really quite distinctive when inspected closely.

Behavior　In the summer, these bats live in a variety of crevices, such as under tree bark, in woodpecker holes, or in other tree hollows. Individuals occasionally appear in buildings, but even then they prefer open sheds, garages, and outbuildings instead of enclosed places.

Silver-haired bats emerge earlier in the evening than most bats and are among the slowest of flyers. They usually forage over woodland ponds and streams and sometimes in forest clearings, often quite low. They feed on a wide variety of small insects.

Little is known about their migratory and hibernation behavior. They frequently collide with radio towers and high-rise buildings during their fall migration, which is often in the company of red bats and small birds. In Tennessee, I found them hibernating in deep cliff-face crevices and observed them to be one of the area's most abundant bats in April, though all but a few males disappeared by summer. They are most likely to be found by people during migration, or in southern areas during hibernation. They are often found in spaces between piles of lumber or firewood, sometimes even beneath rocks.

Seasonal, geographic segregation of the sexes is also likely in this species. In summer, only males have been found in Arizona, New Mexico, South Carolina, and Tennessee, while nearly all adults sampled in the Adirondack Mountains were females.

Nursery colonies appear to be formed only in the northern United States and Canada. Very few of these have been found, but available evidence indicates that they range from a few dozen to thousands of individuals in rare instances.

Their breeding behavior remains largely unknown, though it likely is similar to other temperate-zone bats that mate in the fall. Twins are born in late June or early July.

Importance to Humans   Silver-haired bats rarely cause a problem. As with most other tree-dwelling bats, public health problems would be virtually nonexistent if people would simply leave them alone. Although unstudied, their insectivorous feeding habits are undoubtedly beneficial.

Distribution of the silver-haired bat (Lasionycteris noctivagans).

Silver-haired bats often roost in bark crevices on tree trunks, especially during migration. Their unique coloration blends well, making them difficult to find.

GLOSSARY

Anticoagulant A substance that hinders the clotting of blood.

Asymptomatic carrier An animal that can contract a disease and transmit it to other animals without showing symptoms itself.

Bachelor colony A colony of bats composed mostly of males and nonbreeding females.

Bird netting A durable, often polypropylene, netting material used primarily to protect fruit trees so that birds cannot take ripe fruit before the harvest. It also is increasingly used to exclude bats from buildings.

Chiroptera The order of mammals that includes all bats. The word literally means "hand-wing." These are the only true flying mammals.

Copulation The act of sexual intercourse.

Echolocation The use of reflected sound from an emitter (such as a bat or dolphin) to locate objects.

Flying foxes Bats of the suborder Megachiroptera, family Pteropodidae, especially the ones belonging to the genus *Pteropus*. They all have large eyes, eat primarily fruit or nectar, and generally lack echolocation ability. They live only in tropical and subtropical climates of the Old World.

Forearm The part of the arm between the elbow and wrist. In a bat it is enclosed in the wing membrane and is the largest bone. It is measured when the wing is folded parallel to the bat's body.

Fungus Fungii include molds, rusts, mildews, smuts, mushrooms, and yeasts. They lack chlorophyll and live as parasites or by feeding on other organic matter.

Gestation period The period from conception to birth; that is, when the mother is pregnant.

Guano Bat excrement or droppings, sometimes used as fertilizer.

Hibernation A state of greatly reduced activity and metabolism produced by the lowering of body temperature. It occurs in winter, enabling an animal to survive on stored fat reserves until spring.

House bats All bat species that frequently roost in buildings.

Keystone species Any plant or animal that is especially important to the survival of many other species. Without it the others would become extinct.

Megachiroptera One of the two suborders of Chiroptera, including a single family, the Pteropodidae. *See* Flying foxes.

Microchiroptera One of the two suborders of Chiroptera. It includes 17 families of mostly small insect-eating bats. All bats living in the United States and Canada belong to this group.

Monogamous Having only one mate at a time.

Nose leaf The fleshy flap of skin around the nostrils of some bats. In American species it is usually triangular and rises vertically from above the tip of the nose.

Nursery colony A group of pregnant or nursing bats that gather into a single large colony, sometimes hundreds or even millions, for the purpose of rearing young. The shared body heat is essential to growth of the young.

Parasite An organism living off energy provided by a host that receives no compensation. For bats and other mammals these include mostly fleas, mites, ticks, and biting flies externally and worms, flukes, and other small organisms internally.

Pectoral Located on the chest.

Sampling bias A sample is biased if it is not representative of the population being sampled. For example, in bat populations the actual incidence of rabies is usually about a half of 1 percent or less, but samples often indicate a much higher level of infection. That is because sick bats are more easily captured than healthy ones. The bias is toward a higher infection rate than actually exists in real populations. Frequently the figures reported in the general media are based on highly biased "samples" of sick, rabies-suspect bats, not statistically accurate samples from normal populations. Unfortunately, the results often are reported as though they represent natural populations of all bats.

Seed dispersal   The act of transporting seeds from the parent plant to new locations where they are more likely to survive. When forests are cleared they cannot regenerate without such activities.

Tail membrane   The membrane that spans the area between a bat's legs, feet, and tail, often referred to as the interfemoral membrane.

Torpor   A state of reduced activity and metabolism similar to hibernation but not necessarily associated with a particular season. Many bats, unlike most other mammals, can enter torpor to save energy at almost any time.

Tracking powder   A powder, usually an anticoagulant poison, spread where rats or mice will step on it and be killed by absorbing it through their skin.

Tragus   A flap of skin at the base of the external ear. It often rises vertically like a small sword.

Tree bats   Bats that roost primarily in trees. Most of these live in foliage, some beneath bark, and others in hollows. Some species that once roosted in tree hollows have been forced to switch to buildings because of a scarcity of old, hollow trees and are more likely now to be referred to as "house" bats.

Ultrasonic   Having a frequency above the human ear's audibility limit of about 20,000 cycles per second.

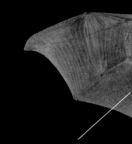

Wing membrane

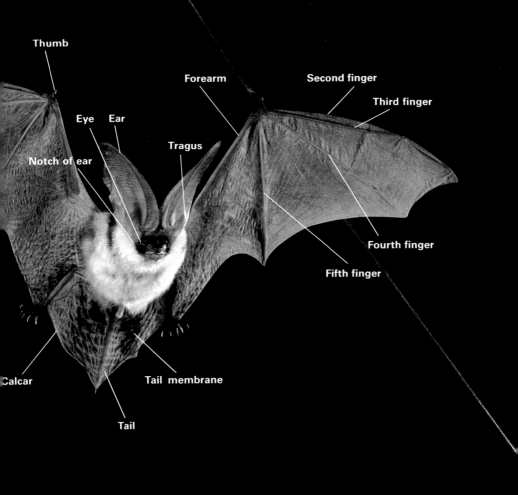

Thumb

Forearm

Second finger

Third finger

Eye **Ear**

Tragus

Notch of ear

Fourth finger

Fifth finger

Calcar

Tail membrane

Tail

Major structural features of a
bat. Shown here is the spotted
bat (Euderma maculatum), *of*
the southwestern United
States.

A BEGINNER'S KEY
TO AMERICAN BATS

The following key should enable interested persons to identify common North American bats or, at least, to assign them to the proper groups. No bat should be handled by a novice without use of leather work gloves. The largest group of bats consists of the 14 species of mouse-eared bats, a group containing several kinds that even experts often have a difficult time identifying in the field. For the best key that includes all North American species (north of Mexico), see *Bats of America* by Roger W. Barbour and Wayne H. Davis.

To identify a bat, obtain a millimeter ruler to make required measurements and simply choose the appropriate alternative for each pair of numbers (1,1; 2,2; etc.), beginning with 1,1 and continuing (as directed by the number at the end of each line) until you end up with a name at the end of the line instead of a number. It may be helpful to remember that bats in the families Phyllostomidae and Mormoopidae are found only in the southwestern United States, mostly near the Mexican border.

California leaf-nosed bat.

Mexican long-tongued bat.

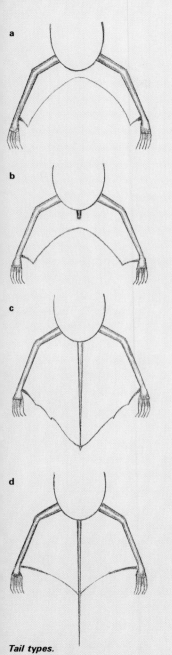

a

b

c

d

Tail types.

1. Prominent, triangular-shaped nose leaf on tip of nose . . . Family Phyllostomidae 2

 2. Ears and tail more than 25 mm long . . . . California leaf-nosed bat (*Macrotus californicus*)

 2. Ears and tail less than 20 mm 3

  3. Tail absent. . . . . . . Long-tongued bats (*Leptonycteris nivalis* and *L. sanborni*)

  3. Tail tiny, less than 5 mm . . . . . Mexican hognosed bat (*Choeronycteris mexicana*)

1. Nose leaf absent 4

 4. Prominent grooves and flaps on chin . . . . Family Mormoopidae, Peter's ghost-faced bat (*Mormoops megalophylla*)

 4. No notable grooves or flaps on chin; lumps above nose or wrinkled lips possible, most faces lacking even these characteristics 5

5. Tail entirely enclosed in the tail (interfemoral) membrane, Family Vespertilionidae 6

5. Tail not entirely enclosed in tail membrane, about one-third projecting freely beyond membrane, Family Molossidae 21

 6. Tail membrane densely furred across entire upper surface, distinct white patches of fur on wrists 7

 6. Tail membrane unfurred for at least the posterior half, no white patches or fur on wrists 9

7. Fur color black with white tips, giving overall frosted or hoary appearance, ears contrastingly edged in black, forearm length 46–58 mm . . . . Hoary bat (*Lasiurus cinereus*)

7. Fur color not black with white tips, no distinctive marking on ears, forearm length 35–45 mm . . . 8

 8. Fur color bright orange to yellowish brown . . . . Red bat (*Lasiurus borealis*)

 8. Fur color deep mahogany, sometimes tipped with silver . . . . Seminole bat (*Lasiurus seminolus*)

9. Tail membrane densely furred on anterior half only 10

9. Tail membrane bare except for scattered hairs along body 12

   10. Color black or very dark brown, dorsal hairs silver tipped, sometimes yellowish tipped . . . . . . Silver-haired bat (*Lasionycteris noctivagans*)

   10. Color yellowish, sometimes ranging from yellowish orange to brownish or nearly gray 11

11. Total length (tip of nose to tip of tail) less than 120 mm, range southwestern United States and extreme southeastern Texas , . . . Southern yellow bat (*Lasiurus ega*)

11. Total length more than 120 mm, range southeastern United States through extreme southeastern Texas . . . Northern yellow bat (*Lasiurus intermedius*)

   12. Ears more than 28 mm from notch to tip 13

   12. Ears less than 26 mm from notch to tip . . . 15

13. Fur on back black with three large white spots . . . . Spotted bat (*Euderma maculatum*)

13. Fur on back gray to brown or light yellowish, no distinctive markings 14

   14. Dorsal fur darkest at base, color gray to brown . . . . Big-eared bats (*Plecotus,* three species)

   14. Dorsal fur lightest at base, color pale yellowish . . . . Pallid bat (*Antrozous pallidus*)

15. Dorsal fur tricolored when parted (individual hairs nearly black at base, followed by a wide band of light yellowish brown, and tipped with a slightly darker contrasting color) . . . . . . Eastern pipistrelle (*Pipistrellus subflavus*)

15. Dorsal fur bicolored or unicolored 16

   16. Dorsal fur unicolored when parted (individual hairs one color from base to tip) . . . Gray bat (*Myotis grisescens*)

a

b

Calcar types.

Mouse-eared bat.

Western pipistrelle.

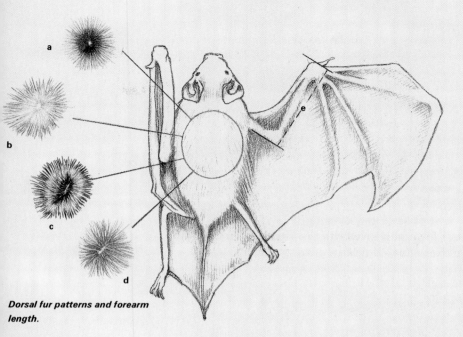

Dorsal fur patterns and forearm length.

Evening bat.

Mexican free-tailed bat.

16. Dorsal fur distinctly bicolored when parted (individual hairs dark at base, lighter at tips) 17

17. Forearm length less than 42 mm 19

17. Forearm length more than 42 mm 18

18. Calcar not keeled, found only in Arizona, Kansas, New Mexico, Oklahoma, and Texas . . . . Cave bat (*Myotis velifer*)

18. Calcar keeled . . . . . Big brown bat (*Eptesicus fuscus*)

19. Tragus rounded, less than 6 mm long 20

19. Tragus pointed, more than 6 mm long, forearms 29–41 mm, color varying from brown or gray to russet, with or without distinctive facial markings . . . Mouse-eared bats (*Myotis*, 13 additional species, often difficult to distinguish)

20. Distinctive black face mask on otherwise con-
    trastingly pale-colored bat, 27–33 mm . . . . .
    . . . Western pipistrelle (*Pipistrellus hesperus*)

20. Distinctive face mask absent, plain brown
    bat, forearm length 33–39 mm . . . . Evening
    bat (*Nycticeius humeralis*)

21. Lips along muzzle wrinkled vertically, forearm
    length 36–64 mm . . . . . Free-tailed bats (*Tada-
    rida,* three species). Only the Mexican free-tailed
    bat (*Tadarida brasiliensis*) is common in the
    United States.

Peter's ghost-faced bat.

21. Lips along muzzle smooth 22

    22. Range, southwestern United States 23

    22. Range, southern Florida . . . . Wagner's mas-
        tiff bat (*Eumops glaucinus*)

23. Forearm less than 72 mm . . . . . . Underwood's
    mastiff bat (*Eumops underwoodi*)

Mastiff bat.

23. Forearm 72–82 mm . . . . . . Western mastiff bat
    (*Eumops perotis*)

SUGGESTED READING

GENERAL INTEREST
Books

Allen, G. M. 1939. *Bats*. Cambridge: Harvard University Press. New York: Reprint, Dover, 1962. 368 pp.

Fenton, M. B. 1983. *Just bats*. Toronto: University of Toronto Press. 165 pp.

Griffin, D. R. 1958. *Listening in the dark*. New Haven: Yale University Press. 413 pp.

Hill, J. E., and J. D. Smith. 1984. *Bats: A natural history*. Austin: University of Texas Press. 243 pp.

Mohr, C. E. 1976. *The world of the bat*. Philadelphia and New York: J. B. Lippincott Co. 162 pp.

Novick, A., and N. Leen. 1969. *The world of bats*. New York: Holt, Rinehart & Winston. 171 pp.

Richardson, P. 1985. *Bats*. London: Whittet Books. 128 pp.

Schober, W. 1984. *The lives of bats*. New York: Arco Publishing. 200 pp.

Yalden, D. W., and P. A. Morris. 1975. *The lives of bats*. New York: Demeter Press, Quadrangle/The New York Times Book Co. 247 pp.

Articles and Pamphlets

Ackerman, D. 1988. Bats. *New Yorker*, 29 February, 37–62.

Arita, H. T., and D. E. Wilson. 1987. Long-nosed bats and agaves: The tequila connection. *Bats* 5(4):3–5.

Clawson, R. L. 1987. Indiana bats: Down for the count. *Bats* 5(2):3–5.

Fenton, M. B. 1985. Introducing people to bats. *Bats* 2(2):1, 4.

Fleming, T. H. 1987. Fruit bats: Prime movers of tropical seeds. *Bats* 5(3): 3–5.

Heinrichs, J. 1986. Build your own bat house. *International Wildlife* 16(1): 42–43.

Kunz, T. H. 1984. Halloween treat: Bat facts and folklore. *American Biology Teacher* 46(7):394–399.

McCracken, G. F. 1986. Why are we losing our Mexican free-tailed bats? *Bats* 3(3):1–2, 4.

Neuweiler, G. 1980. How bats detect flying insects. *Physics Today* 33(8): 34–40.

Tuttle, M. D. 1979. Bats. In *Wild animals of North America*, pp. 47–75. Washington, D.C.: National Geographic Society.

———. 1979. Twilight for the gray bat. *National Parks and Conservation Magazine* 53(10): 12–15.

———. 1982. The amazing frog-eating bat. *National Geographic*, 161(1):78–91.

———. 1983. In celebration of bats. *International Wildlife* 13(4):4–13.

———. 1984. Harmless, highly beneficial, bats still get a bum rap. *Smithsonian* 14(10):74–81.

———. 1986. Endangered gray bat benefits from protection. *Bats* 4(4):1–3, 4.

———. 1986. Gentle fliers of the African night. *National Geographic* 169(4): 540–558.

———. 1988. *The importance of bats*. Special publication. Austin, Tex.: Bat Conservation International. 8 pp.

SCIENTIFIC REVIEWS

Fenton, M. B. 1985. *Communication in the Chiroptera*. Bloomington: Indiana University Press. 161 pp.

Fenton, M. B., P. Racey, and J. M. V. Rayner. 1987. *Recent advances in the study of bats.* Cambridge: Cambridge University Press. 470 pp.

Kunz, T. H., ed. 1982. *Ecology of bats.* New York and London: Plenum Press. 425 pp.

———. In press. *Ecological and behavioral methods for the study of bats.* Washington, D.C.: Smithsonian Institution Press.

Slaughter, B. H., and D. W. Walton, eds. 1970. *About bats: A Chiropteran symposium.* Dallas: Southern Methodist University Press. 339 pp.

Wimsatt, W. A., ed. 1970, 1977. *Biology of bats,* vols. 1, 2, 3. New York: Academic Press. 406, 477, and 651 pp.

AMERICAN BATS

Barbour, R. W., and W. H. Davis. 1969. *Bats of America.* Lexington: University Press of Kentucky. 286 pp.

Geluso, K. N., J. S. Altenbach, and R. C. Kerbo. 1987. *Bats of Carlsbad Caverns National Park.* Carlsbad, N.M.: Carlsbad Caverns National History Association. 33 pp.

Hall, E. R. 1981. *The mammals of North America.* vol. 1. New York: John Wiley & Sons. 600 pp.

Harvey, M. J. 1986. *Arkansas bats: A valuable resource.* Little Rock: Arkansas Game and Fish Commission. 48 pp.

Hekkers, J., ed. 1984. *The bats of Colorado: Shadows in the night.* Denver: Colorado Division of Wildlife. 23 pp.

LaVal, R. K., and M. L. LaVal. 1980. *Ecological studies and management of Missouri bats, with emphasis on cave-dwelling species.* Terrestrial series no. 8. Jefferson City: Missouri Department of Conservation. 53 pp.

CHILDREN'S MATERIALS

Braus, J., ed. 1986. Bats. *Ranger Rick's Nature Scope* 2(4):33–44.

Hopf, A. L. 1985. *Bats.* New York: Dodd, Mead & Company. 64 pp.

Jarrell, R. 1963. *The Bat-Poet.* New York: Macmillan Publishing Co. 43 pp.

Johnson, S. A. 1985. *Bats.* Minneapolis: Lerner Publications Company. 48 pp.

Kaufmann, J. 1972. *Bats in the dark.* New York: Thomas Y. Crowell Co. 33 pp.

Lauber, P. 1968. *Bats: Wings in the night.* New York: Random House. 79 pp.

Laycock, G. 1981. *Bats in the night.* New York: Four Winds Press. 68 pp.

Leen, N. 1976. *The bat.* New York: Holt, Rinehart & Winston. 79 pp.

Schlein, M. 1982. *Billions of bats.* New York: J. B. Lippincott. 56 pp.

PUBLIC HEALTH ISSUES AND NUISANCE REMEDIES

Barclay, M. R. B., D. W. Thomas, and M. B. Fenton. 1980. Comparison of methods used for controlling bats in buildings. *Journal of Wildlife Management* 44:502–506.

Clark, D. R., Jr. 1981. *Bats and environmental contaminants: A review.* Special scientific report — Wildlife no. 235. Washington, D.C.: U.S. Fish and Wildlife Service. 27 pp.

Corrigan, B. 1983. Misunderstood bats. *Pest Control* 51(8):61–62.

French, T. W., J. E. Cardoza, and G. S. Jones. 1986. *A homeowner's guide to Massachusetts bats and bat problems.* Boston: Commonwealth of Massachusetts. 18 pp.

Greenhall, A. M. 1982. *House bat management.* Resources publication no. 143. Washington, D.C.: U.S. Fish and Wildlife Service. 33 pp.

Hurley, S., and M. B. Fenton. 1980. Ineffectiveness of fenthion, zinc phosphide, DDT and two ultrasonic rodent repellers for control of populations of little brown bats (*Myotis lucifugus*). *Bulletin of Environmental Contamination and Toxicology* 25:503–507.

Kunz, T. H., E. L. P. Anthony, and W. T. Rumage III. 1977. Mortality of little brown bats following multiple pesticide applications. *Journal of Wildlife Management* 41:476–483.

Pybus, M. 1986. *Bats of Alberta: The real story.* Edmonton: Alberta Fish and Wildlife Division. 16 pp.

Strohm, B. 1982. Most "facts" about bats are myths. *National Wildlife* 20(5): 35–39.

Tuttle, M. D., and S. J. Kern. 1981. Bats and public health. *Milwaukee Public Museum Contributions in Biology and Geology* 48:1–11.

Tuttle, M. D., ed. 1987. *Bats, pesticides and politics.* Special publication. Austin, Tex.: Bat Conservation International. 42 pp.

BATS AND INSECT CONTROL

Anthony, E. L. P., and T. H. Kunz. 1977. Feeding strategies of the little brown bat, *Myotis lucifugus,* in southern New Hampshire. *Ecology* 58:775–786. These authors found mosquito remains in 77.4 percent of fecal samples examined and estimated average capture rates to be 420 insects per hour. They also noted that sampling biases may have resulted in an underestimate of the true capture rate.

Belton, P., and R. H. Kempster. 1962. *Entomologia Experimentalis et Applicate* 5:281–288. Belton and Kempster demonstrated that broadcasting batlike ultrasound (50 kilocycles per second) over test plots of corn in Ontario more than halved damage from corn borer moth larvae. The moths hear bat echolocation calls and fly away.

Coutt, R. A., M. B. Fenton, and E. Glen. 1973. Food intake by captive *Myotis lucifugus* and *Eptesicus fuscus* (Chiroptera: Vespertilionidae). *Journal of Mammology* 54:985–990. These researchers reported finding 145 mosquitoes among other insects in a *Myotis lucifugus* stomach.

Gould, E. 1955. The feeding efficiency of insectivorous bats. *Journal of Mammalogy* 36:399–406. Gould estimates an average catch rate of 500 insects per hour for *Myotis lucifugus* in the wild, based on rate of weight gain and average sizes of prey.

Griffin, D. G., R. A. Webster, and C. R. Michael. 1960. The echolocation of flying insects by bats. *Animal Behavior* 8:141–154. These researchers report capture rates of up to 600 mosquitoes per hour by bats of the genus *Myotis* in a laboratory.

Lewis, J. B. 1940. Mammals of Amelia County, Virginia. *Journal of Mammalogy* 21:422–428. Lewis reports that *Lasiurus borealis* congregates in large numbers around corn cribs to feed on emerging grain moths.

McCracken, G. F., and M. K. Gustin. 1987. Batmom's daily nightmare. *Natural History* 96(10):66–73. McCracken and Gustin report that the 20 million bats from Bracken Cave in Texas consume an estimated 150 tons of insects nightly, thereby aiding agriculture.

Makin, D., and H. Mendelssohn. 1985. Insectivorous bats victims of Israeli campaign. *Bats* 2(4):1–2, 4. Makin and Mendelssohn report that when 90 percent of Israel's insectivorous

bats were inadvertently killed, noc-
tuid moths that were originally fed
upon by the bats, became major crop
pests, requiring extensive on-going
chemical control.

Qumsiyeh, M. B. 1985. *The bats of Egypt.*
Special publication no. 23. Lubbock:
Museum, Texas Tech University. 102
pp. Qumsiyeh reports that sac-winged
bats, *Taphozous nudiventris,* congregate around cotton fields, apparently
to feed on the cotton leaf worm.

Webster, F. A., and D. R. Griffin. 1962.
The role of the flight membranes in
insect capture by bats. *Animal Behavior* 10:332–340. Webster and Griffin
report capture rates of 840 fruit flies
per hour by *Myotis lucifugus* in a lab.

INDEX

DATE DUE

SEP 1 0 1992		
NOV 0 6 1992		
SEP 2 9 1993		
SEP 1 5 1994		
OCT 2 9 1994		
OCT 1 1 1995		
OCT 2 3 1995		
OCT 2 5 1995		
OCT 2 0 1995		
DEC 0 7 1995		
DEC 0 8 1997		
MAR 1 5		
DEC 1 9 1999		
APR 2 7 2000		
NOV 1 0 2000		
SEP 1 5 2002		
SEP 0 9 2003		